AF896004

20-Minute
BIBLE STUDIES

in

Psalms

KRISTIN NAVE

HarperChristian Resources

20-Minute Bible Studies in Psalms
Copyright © 2026 by Kristin Nave

Published by HarperChristian Resources, 3950 Sparks Drive SE, Suite 101, Grand Rapids, MI 49546, USA. HarperChristian Resources is a registered trademark of HarperCollins Christian Publishing, Inc.

Requests for information should be addressed to customercare@harpercollins.com.

ISBN 978-0-310-18453-9 (softcover)
ISBN 978-0-310-18454-6 (ebook)

Unless otherwise noted, Scripture quotations are taken from the Holy Bible, New International Version®, NIV®. Copyright © 1973, 1978, 1984, 2011 by Biblica, Inc.® Used by permission of Zondervan. All rights reserved worldwide. www.zondervan.com. The "NIV" and "New International Version" are trademarks registered in the United States Patent and Trademark Office by Biblica, Inc.®

Scripture quotations marked CSB are taken from the Christian Standard Bible®. Copyright © 2017 by Holman Bible Publishers. Used by permission. Christian Standard Bible® and CSB® are federally registered trademarks of Holman Bible Publishers.

Scripture quotations marked ESV are taken from the ESV® Bible (The Holy Bible, English Standard Version®). Copyright © 2001 by Crossway, a publishing ministry of Good News Publishers. All rights reserved.

Scripture quotations marked KJV are taken from the King James Version. Public domain.

Scripture quotations marked NKJV are taken from the New King James Version®. Copyright © 1982 by Thomas Nelson. Used by permission. All rights reserved.

Scripture quotations marked NLT are taken from the Holy Bible, New Living Translation. Copyright © 1996, 2004, 2015 by Tyndale House Foundation. Used by permission of Tyndale House Publishers, Carol Stream, Illinois 60188. All rights reserved.

Any internet addresses (websites, blogs, etc.) and telephone numbers in this study guide are offered as a resource. They are not intended in any way to be or imply an endorsement by HarperChristian Resources, nor does HarperChristian Resources vouch for the content of these sites and numbers for the life of this study guide.

All rights reserved. No portion of this book may be reproduced, stored in a retrieval system, or transmitted in any form or by any means—electronic, mechanical, photocopy, recording, scanning, or other—except for brief quotations in critical reviews or articles, without the prior written permission of the publisher.

HarperChristian Resources titles may be purchased in bulk for church, business, fundraising, or ministry use. For information, please email ResourceSpecialist@ChurchSource.com.

The author is represented by Alive Literary Agency, www.aliveliterary.com.

Without limiting the exclusive rights of any author, contributor or the publisher of this publication, any unauthorized use of this publication to train generative artificial intelligence (AI) technologies is expressly prohibited. HarperCollins also exercise their rights under Article 4(3) of the Digital Single Market Directive 2019/790 and expressly reserve this publication from the text and data mining exception.

HarperCollins Publishers, Macken House, 39/40 Mayor Street Upper, Dublin 1, D01 C9W8, Ireland (https://www.harpercollins.com).

Art direction: Ron Huizinga
Cover Design: Faceout Studio, Molly von Borstel
Interior Design: Jeff Jansen

First Printing May 2026 / Printed in the United States of America

Contents

BOOK III

BOOK IV

BOOK V

Dear Friend,

I'm really glad you're here, no matter what brought you, or how full your life feels right now. Like many of you, I've walked through more busy seasons than I can count, when I've longed to be in the Bible more but felt stretched thin. Often that longing comes from the gentle nudge of the Holy Spirit, but sometimes it's also mixed with a heavy sense of guilt. That familiar feeling of not quite measuring up . . . again.

Recently, a conversation with a friend helped me to see this tension more clearly. She's a business executive, a wife, and a mom of two, and she said to me, "I love that you have time to study the Bible, but what encouragement would you give someone like me, who only has about twenty minutes?"

Her question stuck with me. It echoed the messages I've received from so many women asking the same thing: What do I do with the small amount of time I have? Does it even count?

Some seasons invite us to linger long in Scripture. Others feel nonstop—where "busy" isn't just a phase but a constant companion, and time in the Word is the first thing to slide. Wherever you find yourself today, I want to encourage you with Jesus' words: "Take heart" (John 16:33).

Take heart, because God's Word is powerful. One verse can change a life. Remember Jonah's eight-word sermon (in our English translations) that led an entire city—Nineveh—to repentance? Take heart, because God multiplied a small lunch of fish and loaves into a feast. And take heart, because He is still the same God, able to take our seemingly meager twenty minutes and multiply them into something far richer than we expect.

Is it true that more time in Scripture often brings deeper understanding? Yes. Is it also true that some of us may need to gently and honestly examine what's driving our busyness? Also yes.

But for now, let's come just as we are. Let's trust God's power and grace, believing He is ready and willing to meet us with the life-giving truth of His Word.

As we dive into the Psalms together, we can rejoice that we are growing more like our Savior. Jesus Himself was deeply shaped by the Psalms—quoting them, praying them, and living them out (more on that soon).

I'd love for you to join me in this prayer:

Lord, take my twenty minutes. Open my eyes, that I may see wonderful things in Your law (Psalm 119:18).

In His love,
Kristin

How to Use This Study

This study is an invitation—not to do more, but to meet God right where you are.

We will journey through forty selected psalms, eight from each of the five books within Psalms. Each psalm includes commentary along with reflection and study questions to help guide your time. One of the beautiful gifts of the Psalms is that while they form one unified book with shared themes, each psalm also stands on its own, telling a unique story and carrying its own message.

I learned this firsthand years ago when I began a simple weekend practice—choosing one psalm each weekend to read and sit with. That rhythm taught me something freeing: You don't have to study the Psalms in perfect order or with perfect consistency for them to be deeply meaningful. Because of this, you can pick this study up whenever you're able—whether that's daily, weekly, or sporadically—and never feel behind or like you have to "catch up."

Each study is designed to take about twenty minutes, give or take. Some days you may linger longer; other days you may move more quickly. Both are okay. This study was written with a deep confidence in a God who can take whatever time we bring Him and use it to teach, shape, and transform us through His Word.

To help you get the most out of your time, here's what I'd recommend:

- Begin with prayer, asking God to meet you where you are.
- Read the psalm at least once (more if you can).
- Read through the commentary.
- Reflect on and answer the questions—either quietly in your heart or in a journal.
- Consider how what you've read might shape the way you live, pray, or trust God today.

You'll notice there aren't specific "group questions" labeled in this study. That was intentional. Every group—and every season—looks different. My hope is that you'll feel the freedom to adapt the questions in a way that best serves the women you're walking alongside, should you decide to complete the study with others.

And most of all, whether you have twenty focused minutes or twenty imperfect ones, you are invited to open the Psalms and expect that God is ready to meet you there.

The Story of the Bible . . . Leading Us to the Psalms

I was years into my Bible study journey before I learned the beauty of understanding the Bible as one unified story. Ever since then, I've found it incredibly helpful to pause and review the bigger picture before diving into any individual book. When we focus on one book at a time, it's easy to forget that it's part of a much larger story—one that gives deeper meaning to its themes and purpose.

In the beginning, God created the world and everything in it, dwelling in perfect relationship with humanity. When Adam and Eve sinned, that relationship was broken, and sin entered the world. Yet even then, God had a plan—to redeem His people and restore what was lost. Throughout the Old Testament, God revealed this plan through a series of covenants—relational promises that showed His commitment to bringing His people back to Himself.

God preserved Noah and his family through the flood and promised never again to destroy the earth in that way. He later promised Abraham that through his family line, God's people would be established and all nations would be blessed. After generations of slavery in Egypt, God delivered His people through Moses, giving them His law and inviting them into covenant faithfulness. Though God remained faithful, the people continually struggled to trust and obey Him.

Eventually, the people demanded a king. God established the monarchy, and through King David, He made another promise: that a Messiah would come from David's line—an eternal and perfect ruler (Psalm 89:3–4). Yet despite God's faithfulness and promises, the people continued to wander, disobey, and worship other gods. They lived in a constant tension between God's promises and their present reality—longing for restoration, deliverance, and the coming King.

It is within *this* story—the waiting, the longing, the hope—that the Psalms were written.

Overview of the Psalms

I know we're eager to dive directly into the Psalms. But before we do, I want us to slow down once more and consider a focused overview of this book. We now know where the Psalms fit in the larger biblical narrative, but understanding the book itself will help us read and interpret it with greater clarity and depth.

The Psalms are a collection of poems, prayers, and songs—expressions of both lament and praise—written in response to God's promises and the longing for the Messiah He had promised. They give voice to a people waiting, lamenting, rejoicing, repenting, and hoping, all while seeking to walk in covenant faithfulness.

There are 150 psalms written by a variety of authors. King David is the most prolific, with 73 psalms attributed to him. Others include Asaph, a musician (12); the Sons of Korah (11); King Solomon (2); and Moses (1). The remaining psalms are attributed to other worship leaders or remain anonymous.

The book of Psalms is arranged into five major sections (often called "books"), with Books 1 and 2 serving as an introduction. We will be studying eight psalms within each book so we get an overview of the book as a whole:

- Book One (Psalms 1–41) emphasizes praising God and trusting Him in covenant faithfulness.
- Book Two (Psalms 42–72) centers on God's rule and reign, pointing toward the Messianic Kingdom.
- Book Three (Psalms 73–89) wrestles deeply with faith, doubt, and the tension of waiting for God's promises to be fulfilled.
- Book Four (Psalms 90–106) opens with Moses' only psalm and highlights a plea for mercy, contrasting God's faithfulness with His people's unfaithfulness.
- Book Five (Psalms 107–150) moves toward rejoicing and restoration, ending with an overwhelming focus on God's reign overall.

The Psalms are both wisdom and poetic literature. They offer practical, God-centered wisdom, while also expressing truth through rich poetry. As we read, we should expect to encounter things such as metaphors, imagery, repetition, and even hyperbole—poetic tools used to describe very real experiences and historical moments.

On a deeply personal level, the Psalms are an intimate masterpiece. They give voice to nearly every human emotion and experience and often feel like reading the authors' personal journals—raw, honest glimpses into their souls. The Psalms move freely between the depths of lament and grief and the heights of praise and delight.

What a gift that we get to step into this book together!

> The most valuable thing the Psalms do for me is to express that same delight in God which made David dance.
>
> —C. S. LEWIS

Jesus and the Psalms

One of the most beautiful aspects about the Psalms is that Jesus Himself loved and leaned on them. The Psalms were not just ancient songs to Him—they shaped His prayers, His teaching, and even His final moments on the cross.

We know this not only because all Scripture is God-breathed (2 Timothy 3:16), but also because of how deeply the Psalms are woven into the New Testament. Out of the New Testament's 260 chapters, there are roughly one hundred direct quotations from the Psalms and more than four hundred references or allusions to them. Even more striking, the Psalms were the Old Testament book Jesus quoted most often during His earthly ministry.

In other words, to know the Psalms is to better know the heart and mind of Jesus.

Because of Jesus' love for the Psalms, each study includes a section called *Connect to the Heart of Jesus*. This section is designed to help us trace how a particular psalm points forward to Christ, echoed in the New Testament, or lived out in Jesus' own life and words. It's where we begin to see how the Psalms don't stand alone, but fit beautifully into the bigger story of Scripture.

As we study, we'll see that Jesus used the Psalms to reveal His identity as the Messiah. He used them in moments of teaching and even in apologetics. He used them to affirm the authority and power of God's Word. He turned to the Psalms to face opposition and make sense of difficult circumstances. And perhaps most tenderly, Jesus used the Psalms for both comfort and lament—giving vocabulary to grief and suffering.

This means that when we read the Psalms, we aren't just reading ancient poetry—we are stepping into the prayer life, theology, and emotional expression of our Savior.

We could argue, then, that to know and live in the Psalms is to know and live more deeply connected to Jesus—and to better understand the Bible as one unified, redemptive story centered on Him.

STUDY 1

The Happy One

Psalm 1

KEY VERSE

Blessed is the one . . . whose delight is in the law of the LORD, and who meditates on his law day and night.

(VERSES 1–2)

Pause . . . pray . . . and ask God for help in understanding the passage.

How often do we rush past beginnings, only to discover later that they carried the very theme of all God was doing? (Raising my hand here!) Psalms 1 and 2 are the ideal starting point for our study—not simply because they open the book, but because they frame the overarching themes that echo throughout the rest of the collection of psalms. Many believe that these two psalms lay the foundation for the message and purpose of the Psalms as a whole—and even reflect the heart of God's Word itself. So, in this sense, these first two psalms do more than sing "Welcome!" to us as we begin our journey into the Psalms. They embody the beauty of the entirety of God's Word and His plan for redemption. My hope is that as we start with Psalms 1 and 2, we'll discover—not rush past—the place where God wants to meet us most.

Look Deeper

Open your Bible and **read Psalm 1** at least once.

1. What does this psalm tell you about God: His character, His actions, and what He values?

2. What doesn't the "blessed" one do?

3. What does the "blessed" one do?

Think for a moment about your deepest heart's desire.

If we were sitting at a coffee shop, I bet you'd share dreams about your career or love interests, or maybe about finding security, or being free to travel. Maybe your desires are for family, friendships, or to grow closer to God.

Might you also share a desire to be happy?

Sometimes we hesitate to say that out loud because "happy" feels temporary or even shallow compared to words like *joy*. Our culture often ties happiness to things that don't satisfy our souls.

But our psalm of study today tells a different story. The word ***blessed*** in Psalm 1 is from the Hebrew word אֶשֶׁר (*esher*),[1] which means blessedness, or happiness. The kind of happiness inspired by the Spirit. This is not the kind of fleeting happiness that might come from the surprise of finding a ten-dollar bill in a random spot (though that is pretty great), or even from an epic vacation with family or friends (which is a lot better than ten dollars, of course).

As you read and observed in your opening questions, this blessedness—happiness—comes from turning away from sin and delighting in God's law. And what does that true, godly happiness look like? Well, what the unnamed author of our first psalm doesn't say about blessedness gives us a clue that it is NOT void of difficulty, feelings of saddness, or grief. As we will learn, biblical happiness and sadness are often traveling companions. And let's remember from our introduction to the psalms' historical context: ***Times were rough.*** The author describes a deep-rooted happiness, giving a visual image of a flourishing tree that is rooted deep in God's Word, nourished and fruitful.

---

1 Strong's Hebrew: 835. אֶשֶׁר (esher): blessedness, happiness. (as translated in the NIV, ESV, KJV, NKJV).

How beautiful that we begin Psalms with an invitation into the **pursuit of blessedness.**

Could it be that we need to reorient our definition of true happiness, or maybe even more tenderly, have our hope for happiness reignited and rebuilt upon God's truth rather than our circumstances? Let's answer some more questions.

What Does the Scripture Mean?

1. List the three verbs in verse 1 used to describe the blessed person.

   *

   *

   *

2. What do you suppose is the significance or meaning of this progression?

3. What does it mean to "delight" in and "meditate" on God's Word (verse 2)? How is this different from simply reading or obeying?

4. What does it mean when it says that the blessed—happy—one will yield "its fruit in season" (verse 3)?

5. What makes Psalm 1 such a significant foundational psalm and passage for the entire Bible?

Connect to the Heart of Jesus

Psalm 1 seems to neatly package life into two paths: the blessed one and the wicked one. But life doesn't always feel that simple, does it? Most of us (hopefully) wouldn't place ourselves squarely on the wicked path headed for destruction. But even the blessed path can feel pretty bumpy. We take detours and experience stalls, and our progress is often indirect, maybe even "curvy."

When the psalmist says that the blessed person delights "in the law of the LORD," and "meditates on [it] day and night" (verse 2), I can't help but wonder how many of us have read that and questioned how in the world that's even possible. It's almost ironic in this study as we're here, giving God about twenty minutes, and that already feels challenging. Among busy home lives, careers, school, parenting exhaustion, and everything else, reading "day and night" can land us right back where we started: *That's impossible. I'll never get there. I'll never live a blessed life.*

But then the New Testament enters the conversation—with Jesus.

Jesus steps into the reality that no one has perfectly lived out Psalm 1. Isaiah 53:6 puts words to what we already know to be true: "We all, like sheep, have gone astray, each of us has turned to our own way." And then Isaiah gives us the answer to this problem: "And the LORD has laid on him the iniquity of us all."

Jesus took on the weight of our failure—our inability to perfectly delight in and obey God's Word—when our sin was laid on Him at the cross.

But Jesus doesn't just forgive us. **He also enables us to live the blessed life**. In John 15, Jesus shows us that the path of the blessed one is actually possible—not through perfection, but through abiding.

"I am the vine; you are the branches . . .
apart from me you can do nothing."

(VERSE 5)

Psalm 1 uses the image of a tree planted by water (the source), while Jesus uses a vine, but it's the same idea. He is the source. We're not called to generate fruit on our own—**we're called to stay connected**. And it's from that connection, even in the middle of full schedules and tired lives, that we slowly grow into people who delight in God's Word and carry it with us throughout the day. True happiness is found, not in perfectly walking the path, but in being rooted in Him—**the One who sustains us, grows us, and calls us blessed** as we abide in Christ.

So again, what a place to begin our psalms journey.

Apply & Take Action

1. In what ways—big or small—am I walking, standing, or sitting in patterns that align me with attitudes or influences opposed to God?

2. **Do I truly delight in God's Word** or has it become neglected or simply a habit? What might be barriers in my life or heart that get in the way of delight?

3. Do I see myself as a "tree planted by streams of water" (Psalm 1:3)? Why or why not? **What might be draining my spiritual life,** or what's been keeping me rooted?

4. Who can I encourage this week in their pursuit of true happiness?

Pray and ask God to help you apply His truth to your life.

BIBLE BITES for PSALM 1

1. Psalm 1 and John 15 are two of **more than one hundred botanical metaphors** in the Bible.

2. Psalm 1 is unique and mimics proverbs—wisdom sayings—rather than speaking directly to God (like many other psalms).

3. **Chaff (verse 4)** is the light, papery husk surrounding grain before threshing. Farmers toss the threshed grain in the air while letting the light chaff blow away and the heavier, more useful grain fall to the ground. There are several other places in Scripture where chaff is used to describe the **separating of the wicked and righteous.**

STUDY 2

The King No One Can Overthrow

Psalm 2

KEY VERSE

Blessed are all who take refuge in him.

(VERSE 12)

Pause . . . pray . . . and ask God for help in today's study.

Jesus wins. That is the resounding message of Psalm 2. As I opened the news headlines today—perhaps you did too—and reflected on my own struggles and those of others, I found comfort in the message of Jesus' victory. As we learned in our first study, **the first two psalms give us a framework for the entire Bible**, and today we will get to see God's plan for humanity. So, as I like to say at the start of my Bible study, "Let's do this, Psalm 2!"

Look Deeper

Open your Bible and read Psalm 2 at least once.

1. What does this psalm tell you about God and His character?

2. What does this psalm tell you about the "Son"?

Have you ever pictured God laughing? I've imagined God the Father—creator of all good and beauty—bellowing loudly in heaven as He cracks jokes and laughs with delight alongside us. (And can you imagine how funny He will be? His dad jokes will actually be funny.) I can't wait. But in Psalm 2, we encounter a very different kind of laughter from God. **This is one of only three places in Scripture where God is said to laugh** (see also Psalms 37:12–13 and 59:8). Here, His laughter doesn't sing a happy tune—it's directed toward those who stand in open rebellion against Him: nations, rulers, and people who try to defy His authority. In verse 4, we read that God laughs at them and holds them in derision—not out of cruelty, but because their attempts are ultimately futile.

That might sound harsh at first, but there's deep comfort in it. God is not anxious or surprised by world chaos. When everything around us feels unstable—politically, culturally, even spiritually—**God's laughter reminds us of His unshakable sovereignty.** He's not intimidated, He's in control. And not only does He respond with laughter, He responds with the establishment of a King.

The original readers would have thought God's anointed (verse 2), who is set as king (verse 6) and later mentioned as God's Son (verse 7), was referring to King David, the Israelite king in the line of Jesus. But the New Testament tells us multiple times that these verses are referring to Jesus (Acts 4:25–26; 13:33; Hebrews 1:5; 5:5; Revelation 19:15).

Isn't this just amazing?! We get to be a fly on the wall as God the Father speaks to Jesus in this psalm! (I imagine us as cute flies, by the way.) And the Anointed, **Jesus Himself, tells us that God gives Him power over the nations** and the power to execute judgment. In other words, *Jesus wins.*

And in a somewhat surprising plot twist, the psalm ends by inviting the leaders (and essentially, us) into a message of incredible mercy and grace, a place of refuge from the judgment.

Let's study more.

What Does the Scripture Mean?

1. What does verse 3 reveal about the heart of what the leaders and people are rebelling against? What does this tell us about humanity?

2. From what we learned about the context of the Psalms in the introduction, who might the nations and the peoples be who are rising up and banding together "against the LORD" (verse 2)?

3. Why are the nations given to the king as an inheritance instead of taken by force?

4. According to verses 10–12, what merciful alternative does God offer to those who might otherwise oppose Him?

Connect to the Heart of Jesus

Did you know there's a prayer in the Bible that made the place shake? The prayer is in Acts 4, where Peter and John led a bold prayer with other believers. And at the center of that prayer is Psalm 2.

This powerful New Testament moment gives us insight into Psalm 2. The believers in Acts 4:25 tell us that the Holy Spirit spoke these words through David. **Throughout the psalm, we hear the voices of the Father and Son—and now we see the Spirit as the one speaking through David.** Psalm 2 is truly a Trinitarian song.

But it's not just theological insight; it's also applicable to our lives. **Peter and John** quoted Psalm 2 to remind themselves that rulers and nations would rise against God's Anointed—Jesus. And what did they ask for?

> *"Enable your servants to speak your word with great boldness."*
>
> (ACTS 4:29)

Psalm 2 became the believers' source of strength. It reminded them—and reminds us—that human threats are powerless against Jesus' reign. One of the psalm's purposes is to give us comfort in chaos and courage in the face of opposition—because Jesus is King. We also find this theme as the culmination of Scripture, reminding us that Psalm 2, like Psalm 1, undergirds the main message of the Bible.

Like those early believers, we have no reason to fear when we speak about Jesus. We can walk in boldness, knowing that God is sovereign and Jesus' reign is our refuge.

Apply & Take Action

1. What hope does Psalm 2 provide in a world that can make me feel like chaos reigns?

2. How do Jesus' words in John 14:6 also connect with this psalm, particularly verses 10–12?

3. In what ways does (or doesn't) my life reflect one who sees Jesus not just as a friend, but as King?

4. Who might God be calling me to boldly tell about salvation through Jesus? How can I pray for them today?

Pray and ask God to help you apply His truth to your life.

BIBLE BITES for PSALM 2

1. Psalm 2 does not list an author, but the New Testament tells us that the author is King David (Acts 4:25).

2. Psalm 2 is quoted seven times in the New Testament, showing us its importance (Acts 4:25–26; 13:33; Hebrews 1:5; 5:5; Revelation 2:26–27; 12:5; 19:15).

3. First Kings 19:18 is another example of how a "kiss" to a leader was seen as reverence.

STUDY 3

Shield in the Storm

Psalm 3

KEY VERSE

But you, O Lord, are a shield about me,
my glory, and the lifter of my head.

(VERSE 3 ESV)

Pause . . . pray . . . and ask God for help in today's study.

For this study, we shift to a psalm of lament. As mentioned in the overview, there are around sixty-five psalms of lament (which is more than 50 percent of the psalms!). Though we might be hard-pressed to find a lamenting song in the top one hundred Christian worship songs right now, the Psalms are saturated in lament and give us the space and even vocabulary to bring our grief and struggles before God. And for a Bible tip as we head into reading this rich psalm, don't miss the historical context provided in the title, as it will bring deeper meaning to the passage.

Look Deeper

Open your Bible and **read Psalm 3** at least once.

1. What actions and roles are attributed to God in this passage?

2. What do you learn about humanity from this passage?

Sometimes it's easy to skim past the historical details of a passage of Scripture, forgetting that the person who wrote it was a real person, with real struggles. Psalm 3 begins with, "A Psalm of David." When he fled from his son Absalom." This should not be overlooked. David's son, Absalom, conspired against his father to overtake his throne to the point that David feared for his life and fled. (If you have extra time, read 2 Samuel 13–18.)

This is a pivotal moment in history—not only within the context of the biblical narrative, but also as a personal invitation to us, readers of Psalm 3. David doesn't compose this psalm of lament from a place of peace or prosperity, but from a situation almost unimaginable: His own son is pursuing his throne—and possibly his life. Calling it "family baggage" might be putting it lightly.

We see that David doesn't waste any time in his lament, crying out not only about his son, but "many" "foes" (verse 1). At this point, Absalom had rallied up a host of supporters to help him take the throne (2 Samuel 15–18). David turns to God with a lament in the first two verses, but surprises the reader with a praise in verse 3 using the powerful conjunction, "but" (NIV, ESV, CSB, and NKJV translations). This is the part of my study when I sing that old *Schoolhouse Rock* song lyric, "Conjunction, junction, what's your function?"[2] So we should ask, What *is* the function of the conjunction "but"?

David is surrounded by enemies, and the situation looks bleak. But he declares that his God is a shield (verse 3). As we continue our study, we'll explore what that truly means—the beautiful, redemptive work that God was doing in David's life.

It's important to notice that even after describing the peace God was giving him, David still cries out in verse 7: "Arise, LORD! Deliver me, my God!"

I love this moment, because it reminds us that David wasn't some kind of superhero who instantly moved past his fears. Instead, we see his humanity. I imagine him suddenly thinking, *Hold up—God, I'm still struggling! Please deliver me!*

So, let's continue our study of this beautiful psalm, with both honest humanity and redemptive work on display.

---

2 "Conjunction Junction," *Schoolhouse Rock*, accessed March 24, 2026, www.schoolhouserock.tv/Conjunction.html.

What Does the Scripture Mean?

1. In practice, what does it mean for God to be "a shield around me" (verse 3)? Is this meant in a physical, spiritual, or emotional sense? Explain.

2. What does it mean for God to be "my glory" (verse 3)?

3. What can we learn about the reality and theology of suffering from this passage?

4. What does this psalm suggest about the relationship between **God's sovereignty** and **human vulnerability**?

5. What is the significance of David bringing up his sleep in this passage?

Connect to the Heart of Jesus

Did you know that **the only time Jesus is pictured sleeping in the Bible is during a storm?** In the familiar story found in Matthew 8, Mark 4, and Luke 8, Jesus is asleep on a boat with His disciples while a violent storm rages around them. The disciples, terrified, wake Him. Jesus then rebukes both the wind and His followers—bringing peace to the storm and challenging the disciples' fear.

Interestingly, in a similar way, Psalm 3 gives us a surprising picture of David sleeping. Though he wasn't on a boat in a physical storm, **David was in the midst of a life storm—surrounded by enemies and hunted by his own son.**

One could argue that the emotional storm David endured—**his own son turning against him**—was even more painful than the threat to his life. If anyone could understand that kind of pain, it would be Jesus. In fact, **many view Psalm 3 as a foreshadowing of the rejection Jesus would later face.** Like David, Jesus was deeply wounded by those closest to Him. Not only was He betrayed by Judas, but He also faced the rejection of His people—a grief He expresses in His lament over Jerusalem just before His death (Luke 19:41–44).

Through both David and Jesus, we see that God can do the seemingly impossible in the midst of life's storms: He can grant us peace—something that feels completely at odds with inner turmoil—and sleep. **God is our shield against the tossings of fear and chaos.** When everything around us feels uncertain and threatening, He offers a stillness that transcends our circumstances. Just as He calmed the stormy sea and sustained David in Psalm 3, **God remains our refuge and rest, even in the fiercest storms.**

Apply & Take Action

1. **Where in my life do I feel surrounded or rejected,** like David did by his enemies and son? How am I responding to those situations?

2. How do I respond when someone or something tempts me to believe, "God will not deliver him" (verse 2)? What does it look like in practice to replace the truth with lies?

3. How can I bring my struggles or difficult situations to God in as raw a way as David did? How can I encourage someone else to do the same?

Pray and ask God to help you apply His truth to your life.

BIBLE BITES for PSALM 3

1. This psalm is the first occurrence of the word *selah* (ESV), a musical term that most likely means "pause or ponder."

2. In verse 8, "deliverance" has the root word Yeshua, which is Jesus' name in Hebrew.

3. David uses military terms (verses 3, 7) to describe God's protection and his plea for justice.

STUDY 4

A Song in the Darkness

Psalm 4

KEY VERSE

But know that the Lord has set apart the godly for himself;
the Lord hears when I call to him.

(VERSE 3 ESV)

Pause . . . pray . . . and ask God for help in today's study.

The late preacher Charles H. Spurgeon titled Psalm 3 the "Morning Psalm" for its promise of God sustaining us in the morning (verse 5). He called Psalm 4 the "Evening Hymn"[3] because it shows us how to set our hearts and minds on

3 Charles Spurgeon, "Psalm 3," Blue Letter Bible, accessed March 24, 2026, www.blueletterbible.org/Comm/spurgeon_charles/tod/ps003.cfm; Spurgeon, "Psalm 4," Blue Letter Bible, accessed March 24, 2026, www.blueletterbible.org/Comm/spurgeon_charles/tod/ps004.cfm.

God in the evening. I also like to think of these two psalms as the place where morning birds and night owls can finally get along because whether we are inclined to look to God more in the morning or evening, these songs show us He wants our hearts and to sustain us in every moment of our lives. **Psalm 4 echoes the foundation laid in Psalm 1, with its vision of deep-rooted happiness found in God.**

But what makes this promise of joy even more powerful is the setting in which it appears: not in easy circumstances or abundant situations but during distressing ones. Let's not miss the beauty in our study today as **we look for joy not as escape, but within God's presence**—not dependent on or shattered by circumstances, **but anchored in God's character.**

Look Deeper

Open your Bible and **read Psalm 4** at least once.

1. What does this passage reveal about God's character, both through what He gives to David and through what David asks of Him?

2. What do you learn about the heart of mankind from this passage?

Unlike Psalm 3, we aren't given historical context, but we can tell David is still walking through difficulty. He begins with another passionate plea for God to answer him, while quickly turning to some nostalgia and remembering how God has helped him in his distress. David's moment of reflection serves as a gentle prompt for us to pause, look back, and remember how God has shown Himself faithful in the past. We are, admittedly, forgetful people. One moment we're enjoying the richness of God's faithfulness, and the next, we're thrown into anxiety, acting as if He's suddenly lost track of us in our current situation. (I'll be the first to raise my hand here!)

We don't know how much time passed between the first and second lines of David's psalm—it could have been a pause of seconds, days, or even weeks. But what's clear is that David didn't let uncertainty linger for long. Before doubt could settle in, he reminded himself of the relief and rescue God had provided in previous times of distress (verse 1). What if we did the same? What if, instead of rushing to worry or fear, we trained our hearts to first recall God's past faithfulness? There's power in remembering—and even more in doing so *before* our circumstances overwhelm us.

You may have noticed a shift after David's prayer. After David starts off crying out to God, he pivots to addressing the people around him. He rebukes them for chasing after false gods and trying to drag his name through the mud (verse 2). But instead of staying in that space of frustration, David grounds himself in a bold truth: He knows God has "set apart his faithful servant for himself" and is confident that "the LORD hears when I call to him" (verse 3).

What began with desperation is now laced with confidence, and the turning point seems to be when David brought that desperation to God.

Let's be honest, though—it's way easier to fire off a reaction to people first, isn't it? To launch into defense mode, craft the perfect comeback, or stress-text a friend before even thinking to pray. (Yikes! Guilty.) But David reminds us there's a better way: Bring it to God first, get re-centered, and then direct people.

David continues to acknowledge difficulties in life and attacks from people, while also holding God's truth as the ultimate power. Let's follow the beautiful progression in this psalm.

What Does the Scripture Mean?

1. Psalm 4 can be divided into four main sections: prayer, rebuke, exhortation, and peaceful confidence. Where do you see each of these elements expressed, and what is the significance of this progression?

2. What does it mean to "love delusions and seek false gods" (verse 2)? What does it mean in our modern context?

3. Why does the psalmist pray, "Let the light of your face shine on us," in response to the people asking, "Who will bring us prosperity?" (verse 6)

4. What do the two references to the evening (verses 4, 8) teach us?

Connect to the Heart of Jesus

There is one direct reference to Psalm 4 in the New Testament when Paul writes, "Do not let the sun go down while you are still angry, and do not give the devil a foothold" (Ephesians 4:26–27). Paul is speaking to the Ephesian believers about what it means to live out their new identity in Christ.

One of the greatest gifts of the New Testament—besides the ultimate gift of Jesus Himself—is how it helps us understand and expand on the Old Testament.

Psalm 4:4 makes Paul's point in Ephesians clear: Anger itself isn't the problem—it's how we respond to it that matters.

Remember that striking scene in John 2, when Jesus flips tables in the temple and even makes a whip? In His perfect humanity, Jesus models having righteous anger in His heart but acting upon it without sin. David and Paul both remind us: It's not the being angry that gets us into trouble—it's when we let it simmer, stew, and turn into active sin. This is the devil's foothold Paul was referencing.

Although David had plenty of reasons to be angry—being shamed by others, surrounded by idol worship (verse 2), and hearing accusations that no good remained (verse 6)—**Psalm 4 points us to the heart of Jesus—a heart that could feel anger without falling into sin.**

Apply & Take Action

1. How do I typically respond to distress? Do I go straight to God as David did, or to something else?

2. After searching my heart honestly, are there "delusions" or "false gods" I am tempted to seek or believe in (verse 2)?

3. Have I experienced God's joy in my heart to be greater than anything else in this world? Why or why not?

4. What other truths about God from this psalm do I need to apply more deeply in my life or share with someone else (as David did in verses 2–3)?

Pray and ask God to help you apply His truth to your life.

BIBLE BITES for PSALM 4

1. Grain and wine (verse 7) are frequently mentioned in the Bible as **symbols of God's provision** and blessing.

2. Psalm 4 is the first psalm that indicates the psalm should be sung and set to music "with stringed instruments."

3. Verse 6—"Let the light of your face shine on us"—echoes the Aaronic blessing found in Numbers 6:24–26.

STUDY 5

Surprising Glory

Psalm 8

KEY VERSE

You have set your glory in the heavens. Through the praise of children and infants you have established a stronghold against your enemies.

(VERSES 1–2)

Pause . . . pray . . . and ask God for help in today's study.

Have you ever stepped outside at night, looked up at the stars, and thought, *Wow, I am so small?* If we could go camping—or glamping, if that's more your thing—with King David, I imagine Psalm 8 would be part of the conversation around the fire. In this psalm, David has one of those night-sky moments, marveling at the vastness of creation and feeling his own smallness in comparison. But instead of spiraling into insignificance, he turns his awe into worship. Psalm

8 shows us that recognizing our smallness doesn't have to lead to insecurity—it can lead to wonder. In fact, David discovers a surprising kind of glory in our place as humans, one so powerful that **Jesus Himself quotes this psalm** in the New Testament (Matthew 21:16).

Look Deeper

Open your Bible and read Psalm 8 at least once.

1. In this psalm, what does David tell us about who God is and what God does?

2. What do you observe about people or humanity in this psalm?

Psalm 8 opens with a bold exclamation of praise: "LORD, our Lord, how majestic is your name in all the earth!" (verse 1). One of the beautiful aspects of the psalms is the variety in how they begin—some start in desperation, others in delight. The last few psalms we studied opened with cries of distress; this one begins with worship. How relatable that is! One day we wake up with a heavy heart, pleading with God like in Psalm 4, and the next day joy and praise are the first things on our lips.

In verse 3, we're given the reason for David's outpouring of praise. He tells us that he looked up—at the heavens, the moon, and the stars—and was utterly overwhelmed by the fact that God is "mindful" of mankind (verse 4). That's no small reflection coming from David, arguably the greatest king Israel ever had (Jesus aside, of course). Here's a man decked out in royal robes, with more fame, wealth, and military wins than most ancient kings could dream of. Yet, there he is, standing in his palace in Jerusalem, gazing into the night sky, and suddenly feeling very, very small.

Commentator David Guzik puts it into perspective: "With the naked eye, one can see about 5,000 stars. With a four-inch telescope, one can see about 2 million stars. With a 200-inch mirror in a great observatory, one can see more than a billion stars." Guzik goes on to note that if you were to hop in a spaceship and travel at the speed of light, it would still take you *40 billion years* just to reach the edge of the universe.[4] Let that one sit for a moment. Suddenly, a forty-five-minute commute to work doesn't seem so bad.

Given all that, it's not surprising that astronaut James Irwin—who actually went to space on the Apollo 15 mission in 1971—came back with more than just moon rocks. He said, "I felt the power of God as I'd never felt it before." Prior to his NASA days, by his own admission, Irwin was not a Christian. But after gazing down at Earth from space, he became a changed man, convinced of God's presence and power.[5]

---

4 David Guzik, "Psalm 8—The Glory of God in Creation," *Enduring Word Bible Commentary*, Enduring Word, accessed March 24, 2026, https://enduringword.com/bible-commentary/psalm-8/.

5 John Noble Wilford, "James B. Irwin, 61, Ex-Astronaut; Founded Religious Organization," *New York Times*, August 10, 1991, https://www.nytimes.com/1991/08/10/us/james-b-irwin-61-ex-astronaut-founded-religious-organization.html.

Now, unlike Irwin, David didn't have a rocket ship or a space suit. All he had was a clear night and the naked eye. But that was more than enough. **One look at the stars, and he was hit by the staggering reality of how vast the universe is—and how humbling it is to be noticed by the One who made it.** We would do well to follow his example to now and then lift our eyes from our many screens and look up at the starry sky instead. The heavens are still declaring the glory of God (Spoiler alert: We are studying Psalm 19 soon.); we just have to remember to look. We will learn that David's humility is magnified in Jesus as we continue to study.

What Does the Scripture Mean?

1. What does it mean that God "silence[s] the foe and the avenger" "through the praise of children and infants" (verse 2)?

2. What does verse 5, "You have made them a little lower than the angels, and crowned them with glory and honor," mean in light of Hebrews 1:14?

3. How can humans be seen as both insignificant compared to the cosmos and yet crowned with glory and honor? How do we reconcile and understand this tension?

4. Why does the psalm end with the same line about God's majestic name?

Connect to the Heart of Jesus

Psalm 8 is powerfully echoed in the New Testament—by Jesus Himself.

The blind and the lame came to him at the temple, and he healed them. But when the chief priests and the teachers of the law saw the wonderful things he did and the children shouting in the temple courts, "Hosanna to the Son of David," they were indignant.

(MATTHEW 21:14–15)

"Do you hear what these children are saying?" they asked him.
"Yes," replied Jesus, "have you never read,
"'From the lips of children and infants
you, Lord, have called forth your praise'?"

(MATTHEW 21:16)

Jesus responds to the religious leaders' indignation with piercing clarity: ***Haven't you read Psalm 8?*** Of course they had. As trained teachers of the Law, they would have known it well. And yet, they missed its fulfillment right in front of their eyes.

I love how Matthew emphasizes the irony. He describes Jesus' actions—healing the blind and the lame—as "wonderful" (Matthew 21:15). The temple is filled with the sounds of praise, not just from the healed, but from the mouths of children crying out to Jesus. And yet, instead of joining in that praise, the religious leaders respond with wicked indignation. The praise that should have come from their lips is instead silenced by pride. It is the children—unpolished and full of wonder—who rightly recognize the majesty of the Messiah.

The scene at the temple becomes a fulfilled prophecy of Psalm 8: **God's majesty is being declared, not by the learned and powerful, but by children.** Their praise becomes a beautiful melody in the face of the religious leaders' unbelief. What David saw prophetically, Jesus brings to life and also lives through His life.

The smallness by which David saw himself and all of humanity is the same smallness by which Jesus entered into this world. He not only welcomes the humblest and smallest of voices into His kingdom, He entered into the smallness of man to show His greatness.

So when we read Psalm 8, we're not just reading David's ancient song of wonder—we're being invited into a greater story, one that finds its fulfillment in Christ.

The sense of smallness David expresses in verse 4, "What is mankind that you are mindful of them?"—captures the humility of humanity. Remarkably, that same smallness is the way Jesus chose to enter our world. He didn't come in grandeur, but in humility—taking on flesh, becoming like us, even as a baby. Jesus' glory is shown not by distancing Himself from weakness, but by entering into it.

Apply & Take Action

1. When was the last time I marveled at the night sky or creation and thought of both my smallness and significance? What would it look like for me to do more of that this week?

2. In what ways do I have a tendency to think of myself too little or too much when compared to God?

3. Who in my life needs to hear about the majesty and glory of God?

4. In what ways have I forgotten or not believed in my significance to God? (haven't brought a struggle to Him, have lived in fear or guilt, etc.)

Pray and ask God to help you apply His truth to your life.

BIBLE BITES for PSALM 8

1. Psalm 8 mentions "according to *gittith*"—a musical term or instrument scholars think may be linked to Gath, a Philistine city.[6]

2. Psalm 8 begins and ends with the same phrase, which is called an *inclusio* in literary terms.[7]

3. Psalm 8 is the first psalm of praise in the book.

6 "Gittith," Bible Hub, accessed March 24, 2026, https://biblehub.com/topical/g/gittith.htm.

7 "What Does 'Inclusio' Mean?", Bible Hub, accessed March 24, 2026, https://biblehub.com/q/what_does_'inclusio'_mean.htm.

STUDY 6

The Voice of the Skies, the Voice of the Scriptures

Psalm 19

KEY VERSE

The law of the Lord is perfect, refreshing the soul.

(VERSE 7)

Pause . . . pray . . . and ask God for help in today's study.

Today, I want to let you in on something special: Psalm 19 is one of my favorite psalms. Now, I know some might say, "Isn't all of Scripture equally important?" And that's absolutely true. But maybe you're like me—certain chapters or verses have spoken to you in a deeper, more personal way.

Psalm 19 is one of those for me. It reflects my own journey of moving from simply knowing about God to actually knowing Him personally. David captures that transition in a way that's not only beautiful but also rich in meaning when we look at the original language.

If there was ever a moment to get geeked out about digging into the Hebrew and seeing how the deeper layers of Scripture unfold, this is it. And I hope, as we explore it together, you'll begin to see why this is such a profound song.

Look Deeper

Open your Bible and **read Psalm 19** at least once.

1. What tells us about God, according to this psalm, and how does it tell us about God?

2. If you were to divide this psalm into sections based on main topics, what would they be?

Have you ever considered that nature might have a voice? Of course, it doesn't speak in words, but according to David, all of nature is constantly communicating—it declares, proclaims, pours forth speech, and reveals knowledge about God, specifically His glory. Some commentators imagine King David, the author of this psalm, standing outside his palace, gazing out over the city, and watching the sunset as he begins to pen these words. As he reflects on the sun—just one element of creation—he is filled with awe.

What's remarkable is that **David was amazed without knowing even a fraction of what we now understand** about the sun. He didn't know it's ninety-three million miles away, or that its light is exactly the right color to sustain life on earth.[8]

Despite lacking scientific knowledge, David was still overwhelmed by the glory of God revealed in nature. We call this general revelation. But then something unexpected happens. After pouring out his awe over creation, he abruptly shifts focus. It's like that person you know (maybe it's you—it's definitely me) who suddenly changes the subject mid-conversation. In verse 7, David pivots from the majesty of creation to the perfection of God's Word. At first glance, this shift might seem unrelated. But it's deeply intentional.

Even more intriguing, he changes how he refers to God. In verses 1–6, the Hebrew word David uses is *El*—a general term for God. But starting in verse 7, he switches to *Yahweh*, rendered as "LORD" in all capital letters in most English translations. (Bible tip: I love noting what form of God's name is used in my Bible!) We might miss the significance of this change, but Hebrew readers certainly wouldn't. It marks **a transition from God as Creator to God as Covenant-Keeper**—personal, relational, and intimately involved. God's Word reveals His will and purposes in what we would call special revelation.

---

8 Jason Lisle, "The Solar System: The Sun," Institute for Creation Research, June 28, 2013, www.icr.org/content/solar-system-sun.

Don't miss David's message here. We can know a lot about God from His creation. Maybe we would be able to know that He is powerful, mighty, intelligent, and vast. But the way **we intimately know God is through His precious Word.** It isn't God's creation that gives you specific wisdom, speaks God's intimate love and voice right into your heart, or tells you God's specific purposes for this world and your life. Only His Word does that.

What Does the Scripture Mean?

1. What does it mean that the Word of God "refresh[es] the soul" (verse 7)?

2. What are some things that God's Word gives or does for us that creation cannot?

3. What does David mean when he asks for forgiveness for "hidden faults" (verse 12)?

4. Why do you think David ends with a prayer in this psalm?

Connect to the Heart of Jesus

I can just imagine Jesus smiling as David penned Psalm 19, marveling at the beauty and glory of the heavens. Not only was Jesus present as David wrote, He was the very One who designed the skies in the first place (see Colossians 1:16–20 and Genesis 1)! You could say David was admiring the original artwork while the Artist stood nearby, nodding in delight.

Of all the wonders of creation David could have focused on, it's fitting—and Spirit-inspired—that he gives special attention to the sun. After all, the sun becomes a powerful symbol of Jesus Himself. Malachi 4:2 prophetically refers to the coming Messiah as "the sun of righteousness," and Luke 1:78 echoes that imagery, describing Jesus as the "rising sun" who comes from heaven to shine on those living in darkness. Coincidence? Definitely not.

This "sunrise" moment in history—the coming of Jesus—is what we've mentioned means special revelation. Hebrews 1:1–2 puts it like this: "In the past God spoke to our ancestors through the prophets at many times and in various ways, but in these last days he has spoken to us by his Son." In other words, God went from writing in the sky to stepping into the story. And while the heavens declare God's glory, Jesus reveals God's heart and is His exact imprint because He is God.

And here's a (somewhat imperfect, but hopefully helpful) metaphor: Psalm 19 can remind us of a dating app. If God had a profile, all of His pictures would be of creation—the stunning landscapes and golden sunsets that leave us speechless. Just from that, we'd probably know He's powerful, creative, and has an eye for beauty. But just like in a dating app, a profile only goes so far. To truly know someone, you need to have a conversation. You need to sit across from them and hear their hearts and share yours. That's what David tells us in Psalm 19 that God's Word does. That's what Jesus does. They don't just tell us about God—they bring us into relationship with Him.

And when we finally hear His voice—whether through Scripture or the blazing light of the Son—we realize: The God who created the galaxies is the same God who wants to be known. Not from a distance, but up close, personally and intimately.

And His name is Jesus.

Apply & Take Action

1. Of all the attributes of the Word that David lists, which has meant the most to me lately? Which do I need more of?

2. Does my life reflect someone who doesn't just know about God, but knows God personally and intimately through His Word? Why or why not?

3. Who in my life needs to know the difference between knowing about God and knowing God? What can I do this week to be a part of helping them know God personally, if they're just starting with prayer?

Pray and ask God to help you apply His truth to your life.

BIBLE BITES for PSALM 19

1. Some Jewish traditions have children who are learning the Torah lick honey while reading the words, so they know the words are "sweeter than honey" (verse 10).

2. Psalm 19 uses six terms for God's Word: law, testimony, statutes, commandment, fear (of the Lord), and judgments.

3. C. S. Lewis called Psalm 19 the greatest poem in Psalms and one of the greatest lyrics in the world.[9]

9 C. S. Lewis, *Reflections on the Psalms* (Harcourt, 1958), 63.

STUDY 7

When God Feels Silent

Psalm 22:1–18

KEY VERSE

My God, my God, why have you forsaken me?

(VERSE 1)

Pause . . . pray . . . and ask God for help in today's study.

Psalm 22 takes us on a profound journey into the depths of human suffering, while also lifting our eyes to the promise of God's deliverance. This is a psalm of lament—one that encourages us to bring our struggles honestly before God, allowing both truth and hope to meet us in our pain. Many will recognize Psalm 22 from the opening line, spoken by Jesus on the cross: **"My God, my God, why have you forsaken me?"**—the key verse for this study. Because this psalm is rich with prophetic imagery and deeply connected to the life, death, and resurrection of Christ, we will explore it over two lessons, allowing its words to sink in deep. Let's let this psalm remind us that even in our darkest hour, we are never beyond the hope of Christ.

Look Deeper

Open your Bible and **read Psalm 22:1–18** at least once.

1. In verses 1–18, what do you learn about God from the way the psalmist cries out to Him?

2. What do you learn about humanity from the way the psalmist cries out to God?

The opening line of the psalm powerfully captures the tension between deep personal suffering and profound intimacy with God. David could have simply addressed "God," but instead, he chooses the deeply personal phrase "my God." In doing so, he challenges the impersonal and distant nature of ancient idol worship, boldly affirming that the one true God is not only real—but relational. Even in one of the most anguished cries recorded in Scripture, we are given a striking glimpse into the closeness David shares with God.

But David's claim on intimacy with God is met with a heart-wrenching question: "Why have you forsaken me?" The Hebrew word translated "forsaken" in the NIV is עָזַב (*ʿāzab*), which means "to leave, forsake, abandon, or neglect."[10] David doesn't just feel forgotten; he wonders if God has actually left him. David is painfully perplexed, because the intimacy with God he clings to doesn't seem to match what he feels in his circumstance. Morning and night David says he cries out, only to feel God is too far away to hear or save him (verses 1–2). Here is a "man after his own heart" (1 Samuel 13:14)—God's heart—crying out with words we would probably feel uncomfortable with if we heard a modern-day leader or pastor speak them. But with a beautiful rawness, and pushing past polite religiosity, David lays his heart bare as a model for us to bring everything to God.

We will learn that this tension sets the tone for the first eighteen verses. In one moment, David seems to be reminding himself of who God is, but in the next, he's expressing his anguish over his circumstances and wrestling with God over His seeming absence. We will see that David truly seems to be struggling to trust, and nearly one thousand years later, Jesus cries out with some of these same words again to the Father.

---

10 Strong's Hebrew 5800, עזב (azab): to leave, forsake, abandon, let go, permit.

What Does the Scripture Mean?

1. What is the significance of the transitional conjunction *"yet"* at the beginning of verses 3 and 9?

2. What is the significance of David remembering the trust and deliverance experienced by his ancestors (verses 4–5)?

3. What are some metaphors David uses in this passage, and what do they mean?

4. What do the mockers in verses 7–8 reveal about their understanding of suffering and faith? How does this contrast with truth?

Connect to the Heart of Jesus

In two of only a handful of passages that cite the original Aramaic language Jesus spoke, Matthew and Mark preserve the phrase Jesus cried out on the cross from Psalm 22, "About three in the afternoon Jesus cried out in a loud voice, *'Eli, Eli, lema sabachthani?'* (which means, "My God, my God, why have you forsaken me?") (Matthew 27:46; cf. "Eloi, Eloi . . ." in Mark 15:34). Matthew and Mark bring emotional power and historical authenticity to this scene while quoting the original heart language of Jesus.

Though our study began in the original context of the psalm surrounding David's life and circumstances, as Charles Spurgeon points out, Jesus is the greater treasure we find in our study by His quoting of Psalm 22:1 on the cross. Spurgeon comments:

> David and his afflictions may be here in a very modified sense, but, as the star is concealed by the light of the sun, he who sees Jesus will probably neither see nor care to see David.[11]

Additionally, Spurgeon calls this psalm the "Psalm of the Cross." He's not saying we should literally forget about David—of course not. But his point is clear: In Psalm 22, David fades into the background like a star at sunrise, and Jesus takes center stage. **This psalm shines brightest when seen through the lens of Christ's suffering and glory.**

11 Charles Spurgeon, "Psalm 22," Blue Letter Bible, accessed March 24, 2026, www.blueletterbible.org/Comm/spurgeon_charles/tod/ps022.cfm.

Psalm 22 isn't just a cry of affliction; it's a prophetic masterpiece pointing us to Jesus. Read these verses again with Jesus in mind and relish the fulfillment of prophecy in Christ alone:

6 *But I am a worm and not a man,*
scorned by everyone, despised by the people.
7 *All who see me mock me;*
they hurl insults, shaking their heads.
8 *"He trusts in the LORD," they say,*
"let the LORD rescue him.
Let him deliver him,
since he delights in him."

(FULFILLED IN MATTHEW 27:39–44)

16 *Dogs surround me,*
a pack of villains encircles me;
they pierce my hands and my feet.
17 *All my bones are on display;*
people stare and gloat over me.
18 *They divide my clothes among them*
and cast lots for my garment.

(FULFILLED IN MARK 15:24)

Apply & Take Action

1. Have I ever felt (or do I feel) abandoned or forgotten by God? How did I respond?

2. Is there something in my life right now that I need to wrestle to trust God with as David and Jesus did?

3. What lessons might God want me to learn from David's response in Psalm 22 when he feels forgotten and abandoned?

We will finish the rest of Psalm 22 in our next study.

Pray and ask God to help you apply His truth to your life.

BIBLE BITES for PSALM 22:1-18

1. The word "worm" in Psalm 22:6 refers to a specific crimson worm (*tola'at*) used in Israel to make red dye. It had to be dried out and crushed to produce the color. This points to Jesus—dried by suffering, crushed for our sins, and through His blood, we are made clean.[12]

2. The fulfilled prophecies from Psalm 22:1–18 are just a small group of the (at least) three hundred prophecies that Jesus fulfilled.

3. The prophecy of the crucifixion in Psalm 22 was especially remarkable as crucifixion was not yet used as a form of execution.[13]

12 Henry M. Morris, *The Biblical Basis for Modern Science* (Baker Book House 1985), p. 73.

13 Laura Geggel, "Jesus Wasn't the Only Man to Be Crucified. Here's the History Behind This Brutal Practice," *Live Science*, April 19, 2019, www.livescience.com/65283-crucifixion-history.html.

STUDY 8

Don't Give Up

Psalm 22:19–31

KEY VERSE

He has done it!

(VERSE 31)

Pause . . . pray . . . and ask God for help in today's study.

In our last study we left off on a heavy note—David's clothes were being split up like they were being auctioned off. It felt dark, like God was silent. But today's part flips the script with a powerful reminder: Don't give up.

Even in that low moment, David doesn't quit. He repeats a prayer from earlier (verse 11), but this time it hits deeper: "But you, LORD, do not be far from me" (verse 19).

That's the thing about David—we have to respect his honesty and determination. He's not giving in to fear or silence. Instead, he doubles down, asking God to stay close.

Look Deeper

Open your Bible and read Psalm 22:19–31 at least once.

1. What stands out to you about God in these verses?

2. What are some of David's significant perspective shifts in these verses compared to verses 1–18?

The shift we just looked into is dramatic, like an emotional whiplash kind of shift. **One moment David is crying out for help, and the next he's praising God** and declaring, He "has listened" (verse 24). I can see myself doing this on any given day; maybe you can relate.

David's shift might feel sudden, even confusing. But here's something important to keep in mind: We don't know how much time passed between these verses. This isn't all happening in real time—most likely David is telling the full story *after* it happened.

David is giving us a glimpse of what it looked like to wrestle with pain, cry out to God, and then experience breakthrough. Psalm 22 isn't just a live reaction—it's a testimony. Though he abruptly shifts to praise—"I will declare your name to my people; in the assembly I will praise you" (verse 22)—we find out why a couple verses later: "For he has not despised or scorned the suffering of the afflicted one; he has not hidden his face from him but has listened to his cry for help" (verse 24). David's feeling of God abandoning him was confronted with the truth of His constant presence. And not only that, but David wanted to be sure others knew that God's eyes are forever on His afflicted children.

But David doesn't just want his church family—"the great assembly" (verse 25)—to know about the deliverance and presence of God. In another surprising turn he broadens his praise and direction to the entire world: "All the ends of the earth will remember and turn to the LORD, and all the families of the nations will bow down before him" (verse 27). While we might casually nod at a God who draws all nations to Himself, this would have been ground-breaking news in the ancient world: Yahweh was not just God for the Israelites while the idols—Baal, Dagon, Marduk, and others—were for the rest of the world.

God was going to draw all people groups and ethnicities to Himself.

David realizes that even in his darkest moment, God hasn't left him, and God is present. That realization was powerful enough that David couldn't keep it to himself—he wanted everyone to know that God sees and cares for those who are hurting.

But David doesn't stop with his own community. In verse 27, he says,

All the ends of the earth will remember and turn to the LORD, and all the families of the nations will bow down before him.

In a world where gods were believed to be local, David boldly declares that God is the God of *all* people.

This psalm reminds us that God is not distant. His heart is for everyone.

What Does the Scripture Mean?

1. What does it mean that "dominion belongs to the LORD" (verse 28)?

2. What is the significance and meaning of verse 29, specifically about those "who cannot keep themselves alive"?

3. How do you think David envisioned future generations would be told about the Lord (verse 30)?

4. What truths does this psalm give us about suffering?

Connect to the Heart of Jesus

Psalm 22 lifts up the pain and power of the cross. It shows the darkest moment—Jesus, the Son of Man, brutally crucified—but also points to the biggest victory ever: His beating death and changing everything. But who could have anticipated perhaps the greatest suffering of Jesus—His feeling forsaken by God Himself and quoting the words of Psalm 22:1? **Charles Spurgeon calls it the "saddest cry from the cross,"**[14] and though most commentators agree that

14 Charles Spurgeon, "The Saddest Cry from the Cross," Spurgeon Center, accessed March 24, 2026, www.spurgeon.org/resource-library/sermons/the-saddest-cry-from-the-cross.

it is hard to fully comprehend what Jesus meant on the cross, Got Questions Ministries gives some insight:

> He was made a sin-offering, and He died in our place, on our account, that He might bring us near to God. It was this, doubtless, that intensified His sufferings and part of why Jesus asked, "My God, my God, why have you forsaken me?" It was the manifestation of God's hatred of sin, in some unexplained way, that Jesus experienced in that terrible hour. The suffering he endured was due to us, and it is that suffering by which we can be saved from eternal death.[15]

Whatever the reason behind this moment on the cross, we can be confident that Jesus understands what it means to feel utterly alone. He didn't just endure intense physical suffering—he also experienced profound emotional and spiritual anguish. And for many of us, the pain of soul-level suffering can feel even heavier than physical pain.

Psalm 22 might be one of the clearest signs that the psalms were deeply loved—and deeply known—by Jesus. As fully God and fully human, Jesus experienced real physical suffering. And according to research, intense pain and acute stress can impair memory,[16] especially in high-trauma situations like crucifixion.

So, the fact that Jesus quoted Psalm 22 from the cross—"My God, my God, why have you forsaken me?"—is powerful. Under that kind of extreme duress, most people would struggle to recall anything clearly, let alone Scripture. Unless, of course, that Scripture was so deeply woven into His mind and heart

---

15 "Why Did Jesus Say, 'My God, My God, Why Have You Forsaken Me?'", *GotQuestions,* accessed March 24, 2026, www.gotquestions.org/forsaken-me.html.

16 Ayanna K. Thomas and Alia N. Wulff, "What the Acute Stress Response Suggests About Memory," Topics in Cognitive Science 16 (2024), 691–706, DOI: 10.1111/tops.12664.

that it came out even in agony. Jesus loved the songs of the psalms, and more so, He clung to them in His darkest hour as a model for us.

Apply & Take Action

1. How does this psalm help form or reveal truth about the difficulties in life I am facing?

2. How do I reconcile my faith when I face moments of unanswered prayer or when God seems silent?

3. Who are some people in my world that need to hear about the message and victory of the cross? What is holding me back from sharing this good news?

Pray and ask God to help you apply His truth to your life.

BIBLE BITES for PSALM 22:19-31

1. Some scholars see Psalm 22 and Psalm 23 as a spiritual progression from pain to restoration.

2. Psalm 22 is also alluded to in two places in Revelation: 11:15 and 19:5.

3. "My heart is like wax" in verse 14 (ESV) could explain a specific medical condition endured by someone during crucifixion in which the heart can burst or cause a heart attack.[17]

---

17 Cahleen Shrier, "The Science of the Crucifixion," Azusa Pacific University, March 1, 2002, www.apu.edu/articles/the-science-of-the-crucifixion.

STUDY 9

The Best Self-Talk

Psalm 42

KEY VERSE

Why, my soul, are you downcast? Why so disturbed within me? Put your hope in God.

(VERSE 11)

Pause . . . pray . . . and ask God for help in today's study.

I know I might sound like a broken record at the start of every study when I say, *This psalm is so good*. But truly, Psalm 42 really is. It opens the second book of the psalter with raw emotion and deep spiritual longing, penned by the Sons of Korah. What we'll quickly see, though, is that this longing for God doesn't come from a place of ease, but from a soul that is deeply downcast—wrestling with sorrow, disillusionment, and spiritual dryness.

I don't know about you, but these moments in the psalms often bring me a sigh of relief. It's comforting to see that even the faithful—even those who earnestly longed for God—also wrestled with despair in the very same breath. Perhaps we could say that the Sons of Korah used their downcast souls not as a barrier, but as a bridge—even leverage—to press further into their longing for God. Let's dive in.

Look Deeper

Open your Bible and read Psalm 42 at least once.

1. What characteristics and names are attributed to God in this psalm?

2. What phrases do the authors repeat in this psalm, and how might this point to the themes?

While the first book of Psalms is largely attributed to David, here we're introduced to a new set of voices: the Sons of Korah.

It's easy to breeze past the names of the authors like they're just irrelevant billboards, but I hope you see that the context of each psalm adds immense depth. The Sons of Korah have a particularly compelling backstory. Their ancestor, Korah, led a rebellion with 250 others against Moses during Israel's wilderness journey (if you have time, look at Numbers 16). God judged them severely—Korah and his followers, along with their households, were swallowed up by the earth. (Can you imagine that scene?!)

But then, ten chapters later, we're given a surprising detail: "The Sons of Korah did not die" (Numbers 26:11 ESV). Why they were spared while others perished, we're not told. Charles Spurgeon reflected on this mystery by suggesting that perhaps God preserved them so they might, in turn, live lives overflowing with gratitude—lives "consecrated to the glory of God."[18] (In less fancy terms, they gave their lives to God.)

Whatever the reason, the Sons of Korah were spared, and whatever led them to write this psalm, we can be sure of this: Their words come from a place of deep dependence, reverence, and longing for the presence of God.

We also find a powerful practice in this psalm—preaching to oneself. As we study this psalm we will see the Sons of Korah direct their preaching to "my soul" (verses 5, 11). The late preacher Martyn Lloyd-Jones had such a powerful word on this aspect of Psalm 42; it's worth leaving here as we go into our study:

> Have you realized that most of your unhappiness in life is due to the fact that you are listening to yourself instead of talking to yourself? Take those thoughts that come to you the moment you wake up in the morning. You have not originated them, but there they are, talking to you. They bring back the problem of yesterday. Somebody's talking. Who's talking? Yourself is talking to you. Now this man's treatment in

18 Charles Spurgeon, "Psalm 42," Spurgeon Archive, accessed October 11, 2025, https://archive.spurgeon.org/treasury/ps042.php.

Psalm 42 was this: instead of allowing this self to talk to him, he starts talking to himself, "Why are you cast down, O my soul?'" he asks. His soul had been depressing him, crushing him. So he stands up and says: "Self, listen for a moment, I will speak to you."[19]

With that in mind, let's step into the psalm and study closely—not only what the Sons of Korah say to God, but what they say to their own hearts. And perhaps we'll learn to do the same.

What Does the Scripture Mean?

1. How does the authors' metaphor of the deer reveal the depths of the authors' spiritual condition (verse 1)?

2. Why might people be asking the authors, "Where is your God?" (verses 3, 10)

19 D. Martyn Lloyd-Jones, *Spiritual Depression: Its Causes and Cure* (Eerdmans, 1965), 20–21.

3. What does "deep calls to deep in the roar of your waterfalls" mean (verse 7)?

4. What do the psalmists remember in verse 4, and why?

5. What is the resolution to the authors' cries?

Connect to the Heart of Jesus

In Matthew 26:38, just before He prayed in the garden of Gethsemane, Jesus told His disciples, "My soul is overwhelmed with sorrow to the point of death"—a cry that closely echoes the psalmist's words in Psalm 42:6, "My soul is downcast within me." It's powerful to see such raw emotion in the psalms, but even more profound to see it reflected in the perfect character of Jesus Himself. And yet, let's be honest—most of us might feel uncomfortable, even shocked, if a church leader today were to express that level of sorrow publicly.

Then, in one of the most unforgettable moments in Scripture, Jesus continues His prayer in Gethsemane, holding both deep emotional anguish and unwavering trust in tension: "My Father, if it is possible, may this cup be taken from me. Yet not as I will, but as you will" (Matthew 26:39). We're not told if the Father responded audibly, but one has to wonder if God strengthened Jesus in His agony. In a sense, perhaps even here, we see Jesus—who is fully God—modeling what it looks like to preach truth to one's own soul in the darkest hour.

Psalm 42 and Jesus give us permission to be honest about our sorrow, but they don't leave us there. Psalm 42 teaches us what to do during it: thirst for God and speak truth to our own hearts when emotions threaten to drown us. And as we look to Jesus—the Man of Sorrows—we see that He, too, walked this path of sorrow and trust, showing us that deep pain and deep faith can exist side by side.

Perhaps you've had your own moment of walking in that tension, where sorrow and trust exist in the same breath. For me, it came after months of lamenting and grieving infertility, followed by the heartbreak of pregnancy and loss. In that season, lies knocked loudly at the door of my heart: *God has forgotten you. You'll never be happy without children. You're less than.* And more. But in the midst of that pain, I had to keep returning to the Word of God and surround myself with people who would speak truth to me when I couldn't see it clearly myself. I had to learn, slowly and painfully, to preach truth to my own heart, too. And praise God that we have the song of Psalm 42 and Jesus' life to remind us of the power of this practice.

Apply & Take Action

1. Am I turning to the streams of living water (verse 1) or something else to fulfill me when my soul is dry?

2. Am I listening to myself or talking to myself lately (as Martyn Lloyd-Jones references)? What truths do I need to tell myself about difficulties I am facing right now?

3. How do I respond when people ask (literally or something similar), "Where is your God?"

4. In what practical ways can I apply the truths of Psalm 42 to my life this week?

Pray and ask God to help you apply His truth to your life.

BIBLE BITES for PSALM 42

1. "As the Deer" by Martin Nystrom (1984) is one of the most popular praise songs of the 1980s and 1990s and was inspired by Psalm 42.

2. Psalm 42 and 43 are so similar that many treat them as the same psalm.[20]

3. There are other instances of beautiful imagery of deer in Scripture: Habakkuk 3:19, Song of Songs 2:17, and Proverbs 5:19.

20 Derek Kidner, *Psalms 1–72: An Introduction and Commentary*, vol. 15 of *Tyndale Old Testament Commentaries* (InterVarsity Press, 1973), 178.

STUDY 10

Calm in the Chaos

Psalm 46

KEY VERSE

Come and see what the LORD has done.

(VERSE 8)

Pause . . . pray . . . and ask God for help in today's study.

When my daughter was four years old we memorized this psalm together. Though I've definitely forgotten how to recite it, I will never forget how powerful the words sounded coming from the sweet voice of a child. **We find ourselves studying another psalm from the Sons of Korah,** and if you haven't done our previous study yet and read the context for these sons, it would be worth going back to. I found that the context brought a whole new meaning to verse 6b, "He lifts his voice, the earth melts." We remember that the ancestors of the Sons of Korah were swallowed up in the earth as it was melted open by God. Whew. But this small piece of context is just one part of this powerful psalm. So, let's do this.

Look Deeper

Open your Bible and read Psalm 46 at least once.

1. What are some truths about God that the psalmist communicates?

2. What do the truths about God communicate about the need and nature of humanity?

A 2024 Barna research study revealed that anxiety and uncertainty are on the rise—particularly among Gen Z. Two out of five Gen Z respondents reported that they always feel uncertain about the future (39%), anxious when making important decisions (39%), and afraid to fail (38%).[21] These are

21 "Generation Anxious: Gen Z More Prone to Fear, Uncertainty Than Older Generations," Barna, accessed March 24, 2026, www.barna.com/trends/generation-anxious-gen-z-more-prone-to-fear-uncertainty-than-older-generations.

remarkably high numbers, especially considering we live in one of the most prosperous eras in history, with nearly unlimited access to media, books, therapy, medication, and self-care resources—many of which promise to help with these exact struggles.

And while some of these resources can be good gifts from God, helpful in their own right, perhaps the greatest antidote to anxiety and uncertainty isn't found in something new—but in something ancient. Perhaps what our generation needs most is found in the timeless truths of Scripture, such as those in Psalm 46.

That same Barna study also showed a correlation between holding a biblical worldview and experiencing lower levels of anxiety and fear. And Psalm 46 offers exactly that kind of worldview—a vision of life grounded in the unchanging character of God. It's a song not just for Gen Z's playlists but for every generation, for you and me (because hey, who doesn't struggle with anxiousness at times?).

Psalm 46 confronts fear head-on in its opening verse: "God is our refuge and strength, a very present help in trouble" (ESV). But the psalm doesn't stop there. It builds our confidence not on shallow optimism or feel-good sentiments, but on something far stronger: the unshakeable truth of God's sovereignty.

The psalm invites us to look at natural disasters—"though the earth give way" and "mountains fall into the heart of the sea" (verse 2)—and at global instability—"nations are in uproar, kingdoms fall" (verse 6) and wars occur (verse 9)—through a biblical lens. That is, to interpret our world in light of Scripture, which gives us clear answers about God, humanity, suffering, and ultimate hope. And even more personally, Psalm 46 assures us that God is sovereign "in trouble" (verse 1)—whatever that trouble may be.

What Does the Scripture Mean?

1. What does this psalm teach us about God's rule and reign and what it means for the world?

2. Though it's often quoted in reference to an individual/woman, what is God "within," according to verses 4–5? **How does historical context give proper meaning to this verse?**

3. How does this psalm speak into specific conflicts that your country or the world is going through? What peace does it provide?

4. What does verse 10 teach us about God's plan, not just for us as individuals or believers, but for the world?

Connect to the Heart of Jesus

Maybe you've seen Psalm 46:5—"God is within her, she will not fall; God will help her at break of day"—on a T-shirt or floating around social media. I know I have. And like many, I've shared that first part of the verse as a word of encouragement for an individual woman.

And just to be clear—I'm not here to throw shade. I've done it, too! But the truth is, that personal, individual-focused interpretation is only part of the story. When you look at the full context of Psalm 46 (as we were encouraged to do in the What Does the Scripture Mean? questions), the meaning becomes even deeper—and honestly, even more powerful.

Verse 4 actually gives us insight into who the "her" is—it's not an individual woman but the city of God. In its original context, this refers to the physical city of Zion in Jerusalem, the place in the Old Testament where God promised to dwell and show His presence.

But that was just the beginning. **Eventually, God's presence wasn't tied to a location—it was found in a person: Jesus.** Jesus became the true dwelling place of God—and now, through Him, that same presence lives in us. He's not just where God dwells; **He is our refuge and strength.** Always with us. Always within.

And here's the amazing part: It isn't just about one person, it points to something bigger. It's about the city of God, which now, through Jesus, includes the collective body of Christ. We're called to be part of a spiritual family, the church. Together, we experience Jesus as our refuge and strength—not just individually, but together.

And though we aren't promised we'll escape every trial, through Jesus, we are promised strength to get through them. He sustains us. Even when the night feels never-ending, Psalm 46:5 reminds us, "God will help her at break of day." That "break of day" literally means morning. Because Jesus conquered death, the darkness doesn't get the final word. One day, the rising sun—from heaven itself (Luke 1:78)—will break through every night we've faced.

Apply & Take Action

1. What is my specific trouble today? How can this psalm provide comfort and truth?

2. Where do I most struggle to believe that God is "an ever-present help in trouble"? (Psalm 46:1)

3. Do I have a hard time being still (verse 10)? If so, why?

4. How can being still connect me to the heart of God for the nations?

Pray and ask God to help you apply His truth to your life.

BIBLE BITES for PSALM 46

1. Many scholars believe Psalm 46 was written during the time when King Hezekiah was threatened by the Assyrian army (see 2 Kings 18–19), after which God delivered His people.

2. Psalm 46 was the inspiration for Martin Luther's hymn, "A Mighty Fortress Is Our God."[22]

3. The morning (as referenced in verse 5) is often symbolic in the Bible of deliverance (Lamentations 3:23; Psalm 30:5).

22 David Mathis, "A Mighty Fortress Is Our God: Discovering the Power of Luther's Original Lyrics," Desiring God, October 29, 2017, www.desiringgod.org/articles/a-mighty-fortress-is-our-god.

STUDY 11

When Grace Meets Our Guilt

Psalm 51

KEY VERSE

Create in me a pure heart, O God,
and renew a steadfast spirit within me.

(VERSE 10)

Pause . . . pray . . . and ask God for help in today's study.

One of the most well-known scandals in all of Scripture—at least for those familiar with the Bible—is David's affair with Bathsheba. Psalm 51 gives us a powerful glimpse into what came after. It was written after the prophet Nathan confronted David about his sin. And while the details of the adultery and everything surrounding it are shocking, what's even more remarkable is what follows: David's raw repentance and God's overwhelming grace.

That's what I hope sticks with us—not just the failure, but the mercy that met him in the middle of it. May that be what lingers after our study of this psalm, because we all need this mercy in our lives.

Look Deeper

Open your Bible and **read Psalm 51** at least once.

1. What actions, roles, or positions are attributed to God in this psalm?

2. What do David's words teach us about the heart of mankind?

If we read Psalm 51 without knowing the backstory, ***we might think, Wow, this guy is incredibly humble and repentant.*** And he is, but getting there took a serious chastening. The full story (worth reading in 2 Samuel 11–12) shows that David's sin with Bathsheba wasn't just an impulsive one-night stand—it was calculated. He slept with her, got her pregnant, and then tried to cover it up by bringing her husband, Uriah, home from battle. But Uriah, out of loyalty to his fellow soldiers and integrity as a man, refused to enjoy the comforts of home while others were at war. So David escalated. He arranged for Uriah to be placed on the front lines, where he was killed. Even then, David showed no remorse—he actually justified Uriah's death (2 Samuel 11:25). Then comes one of the most sobering and powerful verses in Scripture: "The LORD sent Nathan to David" (2 Samuel 12:1). God saw it all. Through the prophet Nathan—who, as a friend of mine once said, was also basically David's therapist—David is confronted with a parable that exposes his sin. It's in the wreckage of that moment—when David is finally convicted and confesses—that Psalm 51 is born.

As deep as David's sin was, **Psalm 51 shows us that God's grace and forgiveness were deeper still.** In one of the rawest and most beautifully written pictures of repentance, David reminds us what unconfessed sin can feel like—absolutely crushing. But when we come clean before God? That's where freedom begins: "Let me hear joy and gladness; let the bones you have crushed rejoice" (verse 8).

It's a powerful reminder: Being confronted with our sin is painful, but repentance leads to healing, joy, and peace. It's like David is living out Hebrews 12:11: "No discipline seems pleasant at the time, but painful. Later on, however, it produces a harvest of righteousness and peace."

I'll never forget a friend telling me how God confronted her through Scripture about her selfishness toward someone—and she was genuinely *excited* about it. She said, "God was disciplining me, which means . . . my Father was talking to me." And that hit me.

In the same way, **David's repentance and God's forgiveness aren't just theology—they're alive on the page.** Psalm 51 bleeds with the truth of someone who's been caught, cleaned up, and set free. David's greatest victory in life wasn't over Goliath, it was over the reign of sin to continue to consume him.

Psalm 51 is heavy . . . but also deeply hopeful. Psalm 51 reminds us that no sin is unseen by a holy God, but no sin is also outside the realm of His forgiveness.

What Does the Scripture Mean?

1. What does David mean when he says it was only against God that he sinned (verse 4)? Can't we sin against others?

2. What does it mean that we are "sinful at birth, sinful from the time [our mothers] conceived [us]" (verse 5)?

3. How might restoring the joy of salvation to someone (verse 12) be a safeguard against sinning?

4. What does David see as enabling him to "teach transgressors your ways" (verse 13), and why?

5. What does it mean that David's sacrifice is a "broken spirit; a broken and contrite heart" (verse 17)?

Connect to the Heart of Jesus

As shocking and weighty as David's sin was, Jesus levels the playing field in the Sermon on the Mount in Matthew 5:21–22, 27–28:

> *"You have heard that it was said to the people long ago, 'You shall not murder, and anyone who murders will be subject to judgment.' But I tell you that anyone who is angry with a brother or sister will be subject*

to judgment. Again, anyone who says to a brother or sister, 'Raca,' is answerable to the court. And anyone who says, 'You fool!' will be in danger of the fire of hell. . . . You have heard that it was said, 'You shall not commit adultery.' But I tell you that anyone who looks at a woman lustfully has already committed adultery with her in his heart."

Guilty as charged; anyone else? I'd like to minimize the ways I've allowed unrighteous anger or lust in my heart (especially when I think of David), but Jesus says these things are just as serious before God as murder and adultery. While the earthly consequences differ, **in the heavenly court, the heart is what matters—and all are guilty**. Jesus isn't raising the bar—He's revealing where it truly is. Sin starts in the heart, and by that standard, we all fall short. But the good news is this: The same Jesus who exposes our guilt also cleanses our guilt through His death.

And in a vivid and poetic plea, David cries out to God: "Cleanse me with hyssop, and I will be clean; wash me, and I will be whiter than snow" (Psalm 51:7). Hyssop, used in Israelite rituals for cleansing (Leviticus 14:1–7), also played a role in the first Passover—it was used to apply the lamb's blood so death would pass over (Exodus 12:22). At the cross, it appears again, lifting vinegar to Jesus' lips just before He declares, "It is finished" (John 19:30).

David's request pointed forward to the ultimate cleansing found in Jesus' blood. Rather than hiding in shame or minimizing our sin, we can bring our brokenness to God, confident that He will wash us clean—not just outwardly, but completely. In Christ, we are made new—whiter than snow.

Apply & Take Action

1. Do I have any sin that has taken hold in my life? What is holding me back from coming clean?

2. Do I tend to minimize my sin and get defensive, like David before he repented—or do I struggle more with fully accepting God's forgiveness, even after I've confessed?

3. How can I personally apply the truths from Psalm 51 this week? Is there a sin I need to repent of and turn from? Is there someone in my life God might be calling me to lovingly but truthfully confront with their sin—like Nathan did?

Pray and ask God to help you apply His truth to your life.

BIBLE BITES for PSALM 51

1. Psalm 51 is one of the Penitential Psalms (along with Psalms 6, 32, 38, 102, 130, and 143), which express repentance and confession and are often used in the tradition of Lent.[23]

2. Verse 5 is the first and clearest expression of the doctrine of "original sin" in the Bible—that we have a disposition to sin from birth.

3. The word "create" in verse 10 is *bara* in Hebrew, the same word used in Genesis 1 and other places of the Bible. But it's something only God does—indicating that only He can bring this kind of transformation and creation.

23 "What Are the Seven Penitential Psalms?" Bible Hub, accessed March 24, 2026, https://biblehub.com/q/what_are_the_seven_penitential_psalms.htm.

STUDY 12

Wounds from the Sanctuary

Psalm 55

KEY VERSE

Cast your cares on the L*ORD and he will sustain you.*

(VERSE 22)

Pause . . . pray . . . and ask God for help in today's study.

We have an ambitious study ahead of us for our focused twenty-minute studies. Psalm 55 is one of the longer psalms, and while we won't cover every verse in detail, we'll draw out a couple of key themes that will help us engage deeply without feeling overwhelmed. As with any of our psalms, this is just a starting point—you are absolutely encouraged to go deeper. Whether it's five verses or fifty, the psalms are rich and worthy of slow, thoughtful reflection.

Today, we're homing in on a theme that hits close to home for many (raising my hand here): **God's faithfulness in the midst of church hurt and broken friendships**. Psalm 55 gives voice to the pain of betrayal—especially when it comes from those closest to us—and reminds us where to turn when trust is rattled.

So let's open our hearts and minds as we listen to David's words, and consider how **God meets us in these very real and often hidden wounds**. There is healing in His presence and wisdom in His Word for how we move forward.

Look Deeper

Open your Bible and **read Psalm 55** at least once.

1. What does the way David looks to God tell us about His character and provision?

2. What do David's experiences and feelings tell us about mankind?

Psalm 55 opens with David crying out under the weight of external attacks—he describes being "distraught" (verse 2), and his "heart is in anguish" (verse 4), overwhelmed by "what my enemy is saying" and "the threats of the wicked" (verse 3). Slander and gossip are painful enough, but David makes it clear that this is more than just verbal opposition—his very life is under threat. Many of us are most likely familiar with David's tumultuous seasons of being hunted by King Saul and later by his own son, Absalom. But what makes this psalm especially compelling—and painfully relatable—is the shift that happens midway through.

There's a plot twist: David reveals that the deepest wound doesn't come from a known enemy, but from a trusted friend: "If an enemy were insulting me, I could endure it; if a foe were rising against me, I could hide. But it is you, a man like myself, my companion, my close friend" (verses 12–13). This isn't just any friend—it's someone with whom David shared life, worship, and fellowship: "With whom I once enjoyed sweet fellowship at the house of God, as we walked about among the worshipers" (verse 14).

In today's terms, we might say: They went to church together. And for many of us, that hits painfully close to home. Hurt within the church—especially from those we've worshiped, served, and prayed alongside—can be some of the most confusing and painful wounds we experience. The pain runs deep not just because of what happened but because of who it came from.

We naturally expect those within the church—especially those closest to us—to reflect the love and character of Jesus. So when they hurt us, it shakes something foundational. Even as I write these words, my heart trembles with the sting of rejection and pain I've personally experienced at the hands of fellow believers. And I suspect I'm not alone. Many of you reading this may be carrying similar wounds. And if we're honest, we also need to acknowledge the pain we may have caused others.

But Psalm 55 doesn't just give voice to that pain—it leads us on a redemptive journey and offers a powerful lesson in how to respond when friendship and church wounds come. Rather than turning to the familiar—but destructive—coping mechanisms like gossip, bitterness, blame, revenge, emotional withdrawal, or escapism (even though David does long to escape (see verses 6–8), he does something radically different: **He brings it all to God.**

Before David even expresses a complaint, he lifts his heart and his voice to the Lord (verse 1). And that's where healing begins. Psalm 55 reminds us that while Scripture never minimizes our pain, it always points us to the One who can carry and heal it.

What Does the Scripture Mean?

1. How do we reconcile David's prayers to "confuse the wicked" (verse 9) and that "death take my enemies by surprise" (verse 15) with the biblical mandate to love our enemies?

2. What did David recall to mind about God in verse 19, and why do you think this would give him comfort in his personal trials?

3. What does it look like to practice being a person who has talk as "smooth as butter" but also "war . . . in his heart" (verse 21)? Can you think of any biblical or everyday examples of this?

4. What does it mean to "cast your cares on the LORD" (verse 22) in a practical sense?

Connect to the Heart of Jesus

It's easy to sometimes read familiar Bible stories and forget about the emotions and experience behind them. **Jesus saw Psalm 55:12–14 lived out in His life through the well-known story and betrayal of Judas.** As part of His inner circle, Judas had been a part of Jesus' most powerful and intimate moments of His ministry. Judas had sat with Jesus when He called the disciples not servants, but "friends" (John 15:15). Judas would have been with Jesus during many of His healings in the temple (Matthew 21:14). Judas had been with Jesus when He displayed one of the most humble and loving acts through the washing of feet (John 13:1–17). In every sense Jesus could not just relate to, but fully experience the betrayal of a "companion," a "close friend," with whom He had enjoyed "sweet fellowship at the house of God" (verses 13–14).

You can't help but wonder—on the night Judas betrayed Jesus in the garden of Gethsemane, as he approached with that infamous kiss and a crowd of armed soldiers behind him—did the song lyrics of Psalm 55 echo in Jesus' mind?

His talk is smooth as butter, yet war is in his heart;
his words are more soothing than oil, yet they are drawn swords.

(PSALM 55:21)

It's a haunting verse—and a perfect picture of betrayal cloaked in intimacy. Judas didn't just betray Jesus; he did it with a kiss.

Whatever Jesus may have been thinking in that moment, we can assume we know what He was doing: He was casting His cares upon the Father. In the garden, overwhelmed with sorrow to the point of death, Jesus poured out His heart in prayer. And though His road led through betrayal, rejection, and ultimately death, the Father sustained Him.

Jesus' endurance through that betrayal isn't just an example—**it's the very thing that qualifies Him to walk with us through ours.** As Hebrews 4:15 reminds us:

For we do not have a high priest who is
unable to empathize with our weaknesses,
but we have one who has been tempted in every way,
just as we are—yet he did not sin.

That means when we feel the sting of betrayal—especially from those we've trusted and loved—we're not alone. Jesus knows exactly what that feels like. And because of Him, we can bring the full weight of that pain to God, knowing He will sustain us. But it's far more than comforting words in a Bible study—it's also power. Through Christ, we're not only able to feel the pain without being crushed by it—we're also empowered to walk through it without sin.

Apply & Take Action

1. Have I ever wanted to escape my problems, like David? What did I turn to when I wanted to escape?

2. What pain, if any, from a relationship am I holding on to right now? Where is the pain leading me—to God or to sin?

3. What truths from this psalm can I apply to my life this week?

4. Who in my life needs to be encouraged by this psalm?

Pray and ask God to help you apply His truth to your life.

BIBLE BITES for PSALM 55

1. First Peter 5:7—"Cast all your anxiety on him because he cares for you"—is an echo of Psalm 55:22—"Cast your cares on the LORD and he will sustain you."

2. Some Bible scholars believe that David was referring to Ahithophel, his counselor who betrayed him while Absalom, David's son, was rebelling against him (2 Samuel 15–17).

3. Psalm 55 has *imprecatory* characteristics—which are prayers for justice for evil and enemies.

STUDY 13

When Fear Speaks, but Faith Trusts

Psalm 56

KEY VERSE

In God, whose word I praise—in God I trust and am not afraid.

(VERSE 4)

Pause . . . pray . . . and ask God for help in today's study.

Our psalm for today opens with some intriguing background about its author, David: "When the Philistines had seized him in Gath." This short note refers to a fascinating episode in 1 Samuel 21:10–15, and though we're keeping things brief for our twenty-minute study, it's too juicy not to summarize.

At this point in his life, David is on the run from King Saul, and in a desperate move, he flees to Gath—a Philistine city that just so happens to be the hometown of Goliath, the very giant David had famously defeated. You'd think walking into Goliath's hometown would stir up memories of God's past faithfulness and victory. But instead, 1 Samuel 21:12 tells us David was "very much afraid" of King Achish of Gath.

Yes—the great giant slayer was afraid.

That alone is a powerful reminder: **Even in places where we've experienced past victories, fear can still find us.** Psalm 56, which flows out of this exact moment in David's life, reveals something deeply human and incredibly relatable—that faith and fear are not mutually exclusive. They can both exist in our hearts at the same time. And in this psalm, **David shows us what it looks like to hold both: to feel fear deeply, yet still choose to trust God fully.**

Look Deeper

Open your Bible and **read Psalm 56** at least once.

1. Find all the phrases following "in God" and "in the LORD" in this psalm. What do they tell us about God or what He does?

2. What are some of David's pleadings to God that stand out to you, and what do they teach you about the human heart?

Psalm 56 opens with a vivid and urgent image: "My enemies are in hot pursuit" (verse 1). This directly ties back to the tense situation described in 1 Samuel 21:10–15, where David is fleeing for his life and ends up in enemy territory. In verse 3, David openly admits what we already sensed from that story: "When I am afraid . . ."

It's a striking moment of vulnerability. And it raises an honest question for all of us: **What do we do when we're afraid?** On my weaker days, I know I'm tempted to turn to distractions, control, or even unhealthy coping mechanisms instead of turning to God.

But here, David does something remarkable. He follows his admission of fear with a powerful declaration of faith: "When I am afraid, I put my trust in you" (verse 3).

That's both comforting and challenging. Recently, my church community group wrestled with this very question: Does having faith mean we'll never feel afraid? Psalm 56 gives us an honest answer. **Sometimes, fear and faith do coexist—but by the power of God, our fear doesn't have to paralyze us.** In fact, it can become the very thing that drives us to trust Him more deeply.

I think many of us can relate to this. In times of fear or trial, we often find ourselves on our knees more than ever. And David does exactly that—but he doesn't stop there. He turns his fear into prayer, his uncertainty into trust, and his anxiety into worship. That's the invitation for us, too—not to deny our fear, but to let it lead us straight into the arms of God.

What Does the Scripture Mean?

1. How do we reconcile David's statement, "What can mere mortals [man] do to me?" (verses 4, 11) with the reality that people can and really do hurt us, physically and emotionally?

2. From what we have learned in previous psalms, are verses 5–7 a cry for revenge, or something different?

3. With the truth that repetition in Scripture indicates significance, what is the significance of "in God [in the LORD], whose word I praise" being repeated three times?

4. What does the psalm indicate that God's Word can do in our fear? How might this truth connect to the last phrase in the psalm, "That I may walk before God in the light of life"?

5. What does the imagery in verse 8 mean regarding the care of God?

Connect to the Heart of Jesus

When we read Psalm 56 and hear David describe his enemies in "hot pursuit" or attacking him "all day long" (verse 1), it's easy to think of Jesus during the final week of His life—on trial, falsely accused, and ultimately crucified. But in truth, the pursuit of Jesus by His enemies began much earlier. From the very start of His public ministry, the religious leaders were after Him—not just to discredit Him, but to destroy Him.

As early as Matthew 9:10–34, they questioned His authority, tried to trap Him in His words, and even accused Him of casting out demons by the power of Satan (Matthew 9:34). This wasn't a brief or passing opposition. Just like David said, "All day long they twist my words. . . . They conspire, they lurk" (Psalm 56:5–6). The religious leaders plotted against Jesus not for a moment, but throughout His entire ministry.

Their schemes were persistent, calculated, and ultimately deadly—mirroring David's words about his own enemies: They are "hoping to take my life" (verse 6). Psalm 56, then, gives us a prophetic window into the suffering of Jesus, whose entire ministry was marked by opposition, yet who remained steadfast in trust and obedience to the Father.

And in one of the most powerful moments on the cross, instead of calling down judgment on those who mocked, tortured, and crucified Him, Jesus prayed, "Father, forgive them, for they do not know what they are doing" (Luke 23:34). It's a staggering picture of grace in the face of betrayal and violence.

That scene brings to mind a difficult season in my husband's work life, when he was slandered, undermined, verbally attacked, and lied about by a coworker. Like David, he wrestled with the weight of injustice and the temptation to respond in the flesh. I'll never forget the day he came home, weary and wounded, and found a wife ready to go full "mama bear" mode (just being honest). But instead of fueling the fire, he looked at me and said, "Honey, we need to pray for them."

Then and there, he led us in prayer—for his enemies.

That moment taught me more about Jesus than any sermon could. It reminded me that faith isn't just shown in public victories, but in private decisions to choose grace over retaliation, and prayer over bitterness. Like David in Psalm 56, and like Jesus on the cross, we are invited to trust God with our pain—and even more, to trust Him enough to forgive.

Apply & Take Action

1. What am I tempted to fear this week? What encouragement and exhortation does this psalm provide for me?

2. What does it mean to me that God keeps "count of my tossings" (ESV) and collects my tears (verse 8)?

3. What can I praise God for in the midst of my struggles?

4. What does it look like for me to practice "walk[ing] before God in the light of life" this week (verse 13)? Is there an area in which I need God to convict me?

Pray and ask God to help you apply His truth to your life.

BIBLE BITES for PSALM 56

1. The term *miktam* in the introduction is unclear, but one possible meaning is "golden," giving precious value to the psalm.[24]

2. In the original language, verse 8 refers to a "bottle" holding tears—**an allusion to an ancient custom in which mourners collected their tears in a bottle as a sign of grief.**[25]

3. While in Gath, **David pretended to be insane** to escape death from Achish, the king of Gath (1 Samuel 21:13–15).

24 "What Is a Michtam in the Bible?" GotQuestions, accessed March 24, 2026, www.gotquestions.org/michtam.html.

25 Adam Clarke, "Psalm 56," Bible Hub, accessed March 24, 2026, https://biblehub.com/commentaries/clarke/psalms/56.htm.

STUDY 14

Finding Strength in the Rock of Ages

Psalm 61

KEY VERSE

Lead me to the rock that is higher than I.

(VERSE 2)

Pause . . . pray . . . and ask God for help in today's study.

Charles Spurgeon powerfully begins his commentary on this psalm with, **"This Psalm is a pearl. It is little, but it is precious."**[26] I hope we would all agree at this point that the beauty of God's Word lies not in its length, but in its depth, and we could say the same for our twenty-minute studies! The shorter psalms—like Psalm 61—are not a spiritual fast-food drive-through. They

26 Charles Spurgeon, "Psalm 61," Blue Letter Bible, accessed October 22, 2025, www.blueletterbible.org/Comm/spurgeon_charles/tod/ps061.cfm.

are a rich, nourishing feast meant to be savored. Though our time may be short, even twenty minutes is enough to give us a taste of the heavenly riches it offers. **Psalm 61 is an antidote for the weary and exhausted soul**—full of hope and assurance in God. A precious pearl indeed, this psalm is a quiet treasure for every one of us who is stressed out or overwhelmed and in need of strength.

Look Deeper

Open your Bible and read Psalm 61 at least once.

1. Observing all the metaphors for God in this psalm, what do we learn about who He is?

2. What does David's human experience teach us about the human heart?

David is not only crying out "from the ends of the earth" but also from the end of himself: "I call as my heart grows faint" (verse 2). The King James Version renders "faint" as "overwhelmed," and both translations reveal something profound—**David has come to the end of his own strength, and the end of himself.** In that place of emptiness, he turns to God: "Lead me to the rock that is higher than I" (verse 2). I don't know about you, but often when I face seasons of overwhelm and exhaustion, my instinct can be to grasp for control, to give in to fear or anxiety. Yet, David points us toward a different response—**he looks to the solid Rock.**

Dr. Tony Evans once said, "Sometimes God lets you hit rock bottom so that you will discover He is the Rock at the bottom."[27] His words echo David's experience: There is grace in reaching the end of ourselves. **It is in that confrontation with our weakness and inadequacy that we can truly encounter God's strength.** And in another one of his let's-remember-the-past-faithfulness-of-God-to-give-us-hope-in-the-now moments, David recalls:

For you have been my refuge,
a strong tower against the foe.

(VERSE 3)

David's remembrance reminds us that faith is schooled in the classroom of experience. Our faith grows as we see God move in our lives, and looking back can provide us the strength we need in the present. I personally keep journals not just to pour out my heart and thoughts but for the moments I have been able to go back and read old entries, remembering all that God has done. One day I took a highlighter to it, highlighting all the prayers God had answered, and I can tell you, it brought me to tears.

---

27 Tony Evans, "When God Lets You Hit Rock Bottom," *Urban Alternative* (blog), accessed October 23, 2025, https://go.tonyevans.org/blog/when-god-lets-you-hit-rock-bottom.

David continues on in the psalm, expressing trust in the "rock that is higher than I" (verse 2)—God Himself, as a "refuge," a "strong tower" (verse 3), and the One who will provide safety in the "shelter of [His] wings" (verse 4). And David gives indication that his strength is growing as he recalls to mind what God has done and who He is, and he ends in such a surprising way compared to how he begins:

> *Then I will ever sing in praise of your name*
> *and fulfill my vows day after day.*
>
> (VERSE 8)

David journeys from overwhelm to praise. Though we don't know if David is writing this song to encompass minutes, days, or months, **he gives us a blueprint for turning our faint and weak hearts to the solid Rock.**

What Does the Scripture Mean?

1. What literary aspects are used in this psalm, and what do they teach us (metaphor, lament, etc.)?

2. What does it mean to "dwell in your tent forever" (verse 4), both to the ancient reader and to those of us now?

3. What does it mean to **take refuge in the shelter of God's wings,** even while we face stress or difficult situations?

4. With what you know of the line of David, how were verses 6–7 literally and/or figuratively fulfilled?

Connect to the Heart of Jesus

To begin: Look up and read 1 Corinthians 10:4: Who does Paul tell us was the spiritual rock in the Old Testament?

Charles Spurgeon captures David's cry to be led to the rock higher than himself with striking words: "I have learned to kiss the wave that throws me against the Rock of Ages."[28] In other words, Spurgeon expresses gratitude for the very hardships that drive him closer to Jesus. He isn't suggesting that we should call evil good (Isaiah 5:20), but rather that we can embrace the redemptive work God accomplishes through life's storms. **Even as the waves toss and batter us, they can become instruments of grace carrying us straight into the arms of the Rock,** who, as Paul reminds us, is Christ Himself.

28 Gloria Furman, "Kissing the Wave," September 10, 2013. https://www.desiringgod.org/articles/kissing-the-wave.

Spurgeon's words aren't a call to just "suck it up" through the overwhelm, stress, and trials of life. They invite us instead to draw deeply from the grace of God—to press in when our hearts are faint and our strength is gone. Perhaps those very moments of emptiness are the means God uses to bring us closer to Him.

God's words to Paul—and to us—affirm this truth:

But he said to me, "My grace is sufficient for you,
for my power is made perfect in weakness."
Therefore I will boast all the more gladly about
my weaknesses, so that Christ's power may rest on me.

(2 CORINTHIANS 12:9)

That is radical.

This isn't just a feel-good and spiritual-sounding verse—**it's the lived testimony of one who has been to the depths of exhaustion and despair,** and there discovered the sustaining power of Christ.

One of my favorite hobbies is collecting sea glass, and I get asked frequently how it is made. Sea glass begins as broken pieces of glass that end up weathered in the ocean. Over many years, waves, sand, saltwater, and yes, rocks break up, smooth the sharp edges, and etch the surface, giving it a frosted, gem-like appearance. **What was once discarded becomes something beautiful**—reshaped and refined by time and the tossing of the waves. I find the most beautiful pieces, tossed among the rocks.

Just as the sea transforms shattered glass into something beautiful, so God, through the waves of our trials, shapes our brokenness into grace-filled strength—until, like David, we find ourselves shifted and shaped, but also lifted and steadied upon the Rock that is higher than we are—*Jesus.*

Apply & Take Action

1. Where am I **tempted to be overwhelmed** right now? My schedule? A circumstance? A relationship? Something else? How can I cry out to God as David did?

2. What would it look like for God to be my refuge right now?

3. Are there things I am looking to for rescue other than God?

4. How could I share the gospel with someone by using a time when I felt overwhelmed or stressed but experienced God's strength carrying me through? Who is that someone?

Pray and ask God to help you apply His truth to your life.

BIBLE BITES for PSALM 61

1. The word for "faint" (verse 2) is also found in the introduction of Psalm 102 (ESV).

2. The word "tent" or "tabernacle" (verse 4 KJV) points to John 1:14 about Jesus, which translates to "He [tabernacled] among us."

3. Psalm 61:6 is like an ancient way of saying, **Long live the King!**

STUDY 15

Everything Falls Short—Except Him

Psalm 62

KEY VERSE

Yes, my soul, find rest in God; my hope comes from him.

(VERSE 5)

Pause . . . pray . . . and ask God for help in today's study.

As we open Psalm 62, we're introduced to a new name—Jeduthun. The introduction tells us that **this psalm was written by David for Jeduthun.** His name means "praising" or "confessor,"[29] which fits beautifully since Jeduthun was one of King David's chief musicians (1 Chronicles 16:41–42; 2 Chronicles 35:15). But his role went even deeper than leading worship. Scripture also calls him

29 "Jeduthun," Bible Hub, https://biblehub.com/topical/j/jeduthun.htm.

"the king's seer" (2 Chronicles 35:15), meaning he was a prophet who received and spoke God's word to the king.

This small detail reminds us of something powerful: **God was intentional in every part of the psalms.** He didn't just inspire the lyrics—He appointed the voices, the musicians, and even the prophetic messengers who would carry His truth through song. And Psalm 62 carries some incredible lyrics, those that encourage us to put our rest and hope in God alone.

Look Deeper

Open your Bible and **read Psalm 62** at least once.

1. What are the names and characteristics the psalmist attributes to God?

2. As mentioned in the introduction, the main aspects of the psalms include poetry, praise, prophecy, prayers, pain (lament), and power (God's). Which aspects do you notice in this psalm?

You may have noticed—or if not, here's a little Bible tip: **Pay attention to repetition**—in Psalm 62, the words "truly," "alone," or "only" (depending on your translation) appear again and again. James Boice points out that in the original Hebrew the word *only* or *alone* occurs five times in the first eight verses (verses 1–2, 4–6 ESV), and once more in verse 9.[30] This repetition is striking.

Because of it, Dr. J. Vernon McGee beautifully calls Psalm 62 "The 'Only' Psalm."[31] Not because it's literally the only psalm, of course, but because its message is meant to remind us to place our hope and rest only in God.

If *only* that were easy, right? I can think of a hundred reasons to worry today *alone*.

David gives us a peek behind the curtain of his life, showing us that he's no superhero (phew!). He faces real, everyday challenges—situations that could easily tempt anyone to fear, stress, or worry. People are attacking him (verse 3), and what might even be worse, he tells us, "With their mouths they bless, but in their hearts they curse" (verse 4). In other words, they are two-faced. Whether it's worse to have outright attacks or back-handed compliments, David knows both are difficult enough to do what we've seen him do before—preach to his heart:

Yes, my soul, find rest in God;
my hope comes from him.

(VERSE 5)

This inner preaching takes root. In a beautiful transition, David looks outward, encouraging others to place their hope in God as well (verse 8). By specifically

---

30 David Guzik, "Psalm 62—My Only Rock, My Only Salvation," Enduring Word Bible Commentary, Enduring Word, accessed October 29, 2025, https://enduringword.com/bible-commentary/psalm-62.

31 J. Vernon McGee, "The 'Only' Psalm," Blue Letter Bible, accessed October 29, 2025, www.blueletterbible.org/Comm/mcgee_j_vernon/eBooks/only-psalm.cfm.

naming two things we are very often tempted to trust—people and money—he reinforces a timeless truth: Our hope belongs only in God.

What Does the Scripture Mean?

1. Using clues from the text as well as other biblical knowledge, what does it mean to find **rest in God alone**?

2. What does it mean in verse 4 to "take delight in lies," "take pleasure in falsehood" (ESV), or "take pleasure in lying" (CSB)?

3. What does it mean to "pour out [our] hearts to him" (verse 8)?

4. What does David mean by comparing the lowborn and high-born (verse 9)?

5. What is the significance of David ending with the exhortation that God rewards those for what they have done (verse 12)?

Connect to the Heart of Jesus

If anyone understands the sting of people's attacks—both blatant and subtle—it is Jesus. He was slandered (Matthew 11:19), misunderstood (John 2:19–21), verbally assaulted (John 8:48), and even deserted and betrayed by His closest friends (Matthew 26). He experienced every form of rejection and deceit imaginable.

It's no wonder, then, that we find this sobering verse in Scripture describing His view of humanity—even toward those who claimed to believe in Him:

But Jesus would not entrust himself to them,
for he knew all people. He did not need
any testimony about mankind,
for he knew what was in each person.

(JOHN 2:24–25)

At first glance, this might make Jesus seem distant or withdrawn—as if He avoided deep relationships or refused to rely on anyone. After all, the verse says He "would not entrust himself to them." But we know that's not the full picture.

Jesus wasn't a recluse; He was fully present among people. He taught, healed, ate with sinners, and called His disciples friends. And perhaps even most startling, He still called His followers to rise above, to serve, to minister, to change, and to grow, even knowing our proclivities to weakness and sin.

For every cut or wound we receive from others, for every painful glimpse we get of the sin that lives in the human heart, Jesus saw far more. And even David, far from perfect, but also afflicted with deep pain, rejection, and betrayal from others (and an inflictor upon others), didn't live and die in bitterness. In fact, in Psalm 16:3 David makes a startling declaration—that all his delight is in God's people!

But David, as does Jesus, reminds us of where their ultimate hope lay: "My soul, find rest in God; my hope comes from him" (Psalm 62:5). They loved, forgave, asked things of, moved toward, and entered into relationships with others, but their ultimate hope was in God. David and Jesus moved past cynicism with compassion, knowing that "with you, Lord, is unfailing love" (verse 12), and only through Jesus can we walk in this kind of love.

Apply & Take Action

1. When and how have people let me down? **Have I expressed my disappointment to God, as David did** (verses 3–4)?

2. Though David and Jesus forgave the wrongs of others, they did not overlook sin or always move toward everyone in intimacy. How can I use this discernment in my relationships?

3. What is some of the richness in my life that God might be increasing—wealth, job opportunities, ministry opportunities, etc.? How can I walk in thankfulness regarding them, but "not set [my] heart on them" (verse 10)?

4. In the face of injustice or wounds from others, what **hope and insight** does the last phrase of the psalm provide me: "You reward everyone according to what they have done" (verse 12)?

Pray and ask God to help you apply His truth to your life.

BIBLE BITES for PSALM 62

1. Jesus echoes Psalm 62:12 in Matthew 16:27, "He will reward each person according to what they have done."

2. Psalm 62 is a beautiful companion to Psalm 61, both highlighting God as our rock (61:2; 62:2).

3. According to 1 Chronicles 16:42, Jeduthun's sons were gatekeepers.

STUDY 16

Make Him Known

Psalm 67

KEY VERSE

May God bless us still, so that all the ends of the earth will fear him.

(VERSE 7)

Pause . . . pray . . . and ask God for help in today's study.

Psalm 67 reminds us that the psalms aren't just for us to relate to—they're meant to transform us, shaping the way we live and inspiring us to be a light to those around us. **God is on mission, and Psalm 67 invites us to join Him in that mission**—whether it's at the workplace, the playground, the grocery store, the gym, or anywhere else life takes us. (Would you believe that for me right now, the dog park is my mission field?) Wherever you are, let the words of Psalm 67 fill your heart and broaden your vision, guiding your eyes outward so that God may truly be known on earth.

Look Deeper

Open your Bible and read Psalm 67 at least once.

1. What does the author hope the nations learn about God, and how does he hope they will respond?

2. How are the nations and people seen in their relationship to God?

The author of Psalm 67 begins by drawing on the words spoken to Abraham by God in Genesis 12:2–3, known as the Abrahamic covenant:

"I will make you into a great nation, and I will bless you;
I will make your name great,and you will be a blessing.

I will bless those who bless you, and whoever curses you I will curse; and all the peoples on earth will be blessed through you."

The psalmist asks that "God be gracious to us and bless us and make his face shine on us—so that your ways may be known on earth, your salvation among all nations" (verse 1–2). In other words, bless us, God, that we may be a blessing!

John Piper remarks on this psalm: "It brings that covenant up to date and prays it into reality. That is what we are supposed to do with God's covenants—his promises. Bring them up to date and pray them into reality."[32] It's not the popular word of *manifesting* our desires into reality, but **it's the encouragement to hope and walk and pray into the reality of His promises.**

In this way, Psalm 67 not only recalls the blessings promised to Abraham but also extends to all people—including you and me—the invitation to join in with God on His mission. Yet, **the author does not approach this mission out of mere duty; rather, it is sung with joy.** The psalm expresses not only the joy inherent in the mission itself but also a desire for the joy of the nations:

May the nations be glad and sing for joy.

(VERSE 4)

Psalm 67 is not a call to a duty-bound evangelism that can feel awkward or pressured. (Oh, do I have stories of making this mistake, unfortunately! You too?) Rather, it is a rallying cry to share God's goodness out of genuine joy—and for the joy of others.

---

32 John Piper, "Let the Peoples Praise You, O God, Let All the Peoples Praise You!" Desiring God 2011 National Conference, September 25, 2011, www.desiringgod.org/messages/let-the-peoples-praise-you-o-god-let-all-the-peoples-praise-you.

What Does the Scripture Mean?

1. The psalm gives **four main purposes of God for the nations**—to know God (verse 2), to praise God (verses 3, 5), and what are the other two? What is the significance of these purposes for all people?

2. How does God "guide the nations of the earth" (verse 4), even though so many nations/people don't follow Him?

3. What does it mean to be **blessed** according to the Bible?

4. Why should God's people being blessed lead to others coming to know Him?

Connect to the Heart of Jesus

Psalm 67 pulls back the curtain on the ultimate purpose of Jesus' sacrifice: that the glory and saving power of God might be known among all peoples. It also sheds light on why believers are not immediately taken to heaven after salvation. Though there is a big part of me that wishes I could have been whisked away to heaven the second I said yes to Jesus. (Anyone else?) Psalm 67 reminds us that **we remain here for a divine purpose**—that through our lives, God's salvation might reach every nation, every tribe, every language. Jesus shed His blood so that all the peoples of the earth would have the chance to hear and respond to the gospel. This mission is not secondary—it lies at the very center of His heart.

In fact, it is the defining sign of His return:

"And this gospel of the kingdom will be proclaimed throughout the whole world as a testimony to all nations, and then the end will come."

(MATTHEW 24:14 ESV)

The surrounding words of Jesus in that passage remind us that it is not the seemingly obvious things that signal the ultimate end, such as false teachers, earthquakes, wars, tribulations, and persecution. Jesus describes them as "the beginning of the birth pains" (Matthew 24:8 ESV). Jesus gives us clarity so that on days like I had yesterday—seeing a famous Christian singer post that Jesus was coming any minute—we can remind ourselves that, *no, not yet.* We are certainly in the last chapter (hallelujah), but His ways must be known to all the nations.

One of the remarkable ways we see the end drawing nearer is through how **the nations are no longer distant or unreachable.** The writer of Psalm 67 longed for God's salvation to be known across the earth—but he could never have imagined the age we live in, where technology, global travel, and widespread migration have brought the nations to our very doorsteps. **Today, the mission field isn't only across oceans; it's across the street.**

Wherever you find yourself—the office breakroom, the grocery store, the playground, the gym, your classroom, or your child's baseball practice—you are, in a very real sense, among the nations. Just this week I started going to a dog park, and after reading this passage myself I thought, *Here we go.* The diversity woven into our daily lives is a beautiful reflection of God's global heart and His desire that all peoples might know Him.

Jesus Himself modeled this way of living on mission in the ordinary rhythms of life. He preached in His own hometown (Luke 4:16–30), offered living water to a Samaritan woman doing her daily chores (John 4:1–42), and brought healing and hope into the intimacy of family homes (Luke 8:49–56). His ministry wasn't confined to temples, crowds, or a social media platform; it happened in everyday moments with everyday people. In the same way, we are invited to live with open eyes and open hearts, carrying the light of the gospel wherever we go, so that all nations might come to know Him.

Jesus not only loved Psalm 67, which was "for the director of music. With stringed instruments. A psalm. A song" (introduction). Jesus lived this song.

Apply & Take Action

1. When I think of being on mission, am I met with feelings of joy, obligation, fear, or something else? How can I move and pray toward a passionate and joyful heart?

2. What is my mission field? Who are some specific people I want to be praying for more?

3. **How have I been blessed to be a blessing?** What has God done in my life or given me that I can use or share and point to Him?

Pray and ask God to help you apply His truth to your life.

BIBLE BITES for PSALM 67

1. Psalm 67 has been nicknamed the "Missionary Psalm."
2. Psalm 67 is a foreshadowing of the Great Commission (Matthew 28:18–20).
3. Psalm 67 also has been called the "Menorah Psalm" because its literary structure is shaped like a menorah in the temple.[33]

33 "Hanukkah and Nature: The Menorah Psalm," Organic Torah, December 7, 2015, https://organictorah.org/hanukkah-and-nature-the-menorah-psalm.

STUDY 17

When Goodness Feels in Vain

Psalm 73:1–17

KEY VERSE

Surely in vain I have kept my heart pure and have washed my hands in innocence.

(VERSE 13)

Pause . . . pray . . . and ask God for help in today's study.

Today we step into the first psalm of Book III a psalm so rich and layered that we'll be exploring it in two parts. On a personal note, this happens to be one of my favorite psalms—if I had to choose, like if someone took away my Bible highlighters and said they wouldn't give them back until I chose my favorite psalms. (But truly, they all could be favorites!)

We'll end today's lesson on a bit of a cliffhanger—a powerful and thought-provoking one, I think—before returning in our next study to complete the journey this psalm invites us into.

This is one of those psalms that makes us breathe a sigh of recognition and relief, because it's so honest and relatable. It gives voice to a question many of us have quietly asked at one time or another: **Why do the wicked seem to prosper while the faithful suffer?**

Look Deeper

Open your Bible and read Psalm 73:1–17 at least once.

1. What is the truth about God the psalmist, Asaph, begins with, and how does the attribute align with verses 2–17?

2. What is Asaph wrestling with, and what does this teach us about the human experience?

Asaph may not be a widely recognized name in Scripture, but we actually learn quite a bit about him. First Chronicles 16 tells us that he was a Levite appointed by David to minister before the ark of the covenant, holding the position of chief among the musicians (verses 1–6). The rest of the book details his duties: giving praise to God, proclaiming His name, relying on His strength, remembering the wonders God had performed, and more. In other words, Asaph was one of the prominent spiritual leaders of his time. Just picture a well-known Christian leader or pastor in our day.

Knowing Asaph's role and context adds significant weight to this psalm. Coming from someone so intimately connected to worship and God's service, we might naturally expect him to begin with a confident declaration like, "Surely God is good" (verse 1). But, what follows is both surprising and profoundly comforting because it is so relatable.

Asaph openly laments the apparent prosperity of the wicked: "They have no struggles," or "They have no pangs until death" (verse 4 ESV). In today's world, it's the modern equivalent of scrolling through social media and seeing perfectly curated images of people who seem to have it all—wealth, beauty, success—yet live in open opposition to God and His Word.

It's like watching someone climb the career ladder through manipulation or dishonesty, while you're working hard, staying honest, and barely keeping your head above water. Or seeing a friend who shrugs off faith entirely—living however they want, indulging every desire—while you're on your knees asking God to heal your struggling but Christ-centered marriage.

Asaph goes on to describe in detail the difficulties they seem to be free from, characterizing their lives as effortless and full of worldly success. He describes his own response to this as so disorienting that he almost "lost [his] foothold" (verse 2). And yet, despite this outward ease, the wicked remain in opposition to God (verses 11–13).

This tension—between the wicked's apparent prosperity and their spiritual rebellion—is what gives the psalm its raw honesty and enduring relevance. Asaph's perspective reminds us that **even those closest to God wrestle with questions of justice, envy, and the perplexing realities of life.**

Asaph laments the prosperity of the wicked, that is, until he "entered the sanctuary of God" (verse 17). With these striking words, everything changes, and we will study his perspective shift in our next lesson.

What Does the Scripture Mean?

1. What truth does the metaphor "Pride is their necklace" (verse 6) look like in everyday life?

2. What does Asaph feel he is doing in vain, and what might this reveal about his beliefs about prosperity and suffering?

3. What does Asaph mean when he says that he would have "betrayed your children" if he had "spoken out like that" (verse 15)? What might this mean for leadership?

Connect to the Heart of Jesus

I like to imagine that if Asaph and Jesus sat down for coffee together (at a café called He-Brews, of course), Jesus would have completely flipped Asaph's view of trials and true prosperity. Jesus entered a world much like the one Asaph observed—one dominated by characters like the Pharisees, who lived in luxury, exploited the poor, and equated outward prosperity with God's favor. But Jesus called them out boldly:

"Beware of the teachers of the law. They like to walk around in flowing robes and love to be greeted with respect in the marketplaces and have the most important seats in the synagogues and the places of honor at banquets. They devour widows' houses and for a show make lengthy prayers. These men will be punished most severely."

(LUKE 20:46–47)

Their spiritual exploitation, Jesus would have told Asaph, was far more serious than the outward rejection of God he had seen among the wicked. But then, leaning in over a steaming cup, I imagine Jesus giving Asaph a one-on-one recap of the Sermon on the Mount, explaining what true blessedness really looks like.

It wasn't defined by circumstantial wealth or worldly success. Instead, the truly blessed were those "poor in spirit" and "meek," those who hungered and thirsted for righteousness, for they would be "filled" (Matthew 5:3–6).

And here's where Asaph's mind might have truly been blown: Suffering for the sake of righteousness wasn't a mark of failure—it was blessedness.

"Blessed are you when people insult you,
persecute you and falsely say all kinds of evil
against you because of me. Rejoice and be glad,
because great your reward is in heaven."

(MATTHEW 5:11–12)

Even when hardship seems endless, when our faithfulness seems only to bring more trials, Jesus provides comfort and perspective:

"In this world you will have trouble.
But take heart! I have overcome the world."

(JOHN 16:33)

In that café conversation, Asaph would have learned that prosperity and blessing are not measured by what the world sees, but by the heart aligned with God, the courage to endure trials, and the hope of the eternal reward that Jesus Himself guarantees.

Apply & Take Action

1. Are there aspects of a life without God that I am envying, or that seem easier?

2. Have I ever felt like my faithfulness to God in an area was in vain? How did I respond to that feeling?

3. How can I be encouraged today by Asaph's raw honesty? How can I be a safer person for others to be brutally honest with?

Pray and ask God to help you apply His truth to your life.

BIBLE BITES for PSALM 73:1-17

1. Psalm 73 is the **beginning of the third book of psalms,** which spans Psalms 73–89.

2. Asaph wrote twelve psalms in total, and one of the most common themes in his psalms is that of the judgment of God.

3. The **sons of Asaph** are mentioned three times in Scripture (1 Chronicles 25:1; 2 Chronicles 20:14; Ezra 2:41) and were most likely comprised of poets and singers.

STUDY 18

When Heaven Meets Earth

Psalm 73:18–28

KEY VERSE

Whom have I in heaven but you?
And earth has nothing I desire besides you.

(VERSE 25)

Pause . . . pray . . . and ask God for help in today's study.

We left study 17 with a powerful transition. Asaph had lamented the seeming prosperity of the wicked, trying to sort out his perplexity of why the faithful seemed to suffer alongside the wicked's prosperity. But he makes a decision that changes everything:

When I tried to understand all this, it troubled me deeply till I entered the sanctuary of God; then I understood their final destiny.

(VERSES 16–17)

The sanctuary represented both the physical place of meeting with God and His presence (Exodus 25:8–9). **The sanctuary was the communal gathering of the people of God as well as where one could meet God personally.** And it's in this space that we will see God do a beautiful transformation.

Look Deeper at 73:17-28

Open your Bible and read Psalm 73:18–28 at least once.

1. What did Asaph learn about God when he went into the sanctuary?

2. What do you learn about mankind from Asaph's portrayal of the wicked and his relationship with God?

Asaph couldn't find comfort by looking at the wicked from an earthly perspective—he needed an eternal one. His peace didn't come from seeing temporary fairness restored, but from realizing the ultimate destiny of those who reject God: "ruin" (verse 18). Though that realization may sound harsh, it gave Asaph perspective—earthly success without God is fleeting, and its end is destruction.

But before Asaph could become self-righteous in that understanding, he was confronted with a painful truth: His own heart wasn't so different.

When my heart was grieved and my spirit embittered,
I was senseless and ignorant; I was a brute beast before you.

(PSALM 73:21–22)

In that moment, Asaph was humbled. He realized he had been interpreting life through ignorance rather than through the lens of faith. **He had elevated outward circumstances above inward communion with God.**

And then comes one of the most beautiful turning points in all of Scripture—marked by a single, grace-filled word: "Yet" or "Nevertheless" (depending on the translation).

Yet I am always with you;
you hold me by my right hand.

(PSALM 73:23)

It's as if Asaph is saying, "I've been bitter, foolish, and faithless, but You—God—have never let me go."

This "Yet" is the hinge of the psalm—as **Asaph realizes there is nothing better than God not just on earth but also in heaven** (verse 25). It's in this realization that Asaph decides that though the wicked may continue to prosper on this earth, he has made a decision:

But as for me, it is good to be near God.

(VERSE 28)

Asaph has seen that there is nothing better than being near to God, even if it means a life of difficulty.

What Does the Scripture Mean?

1. What does it mean for Asaph to be guided by God's counsel (verse 24)?

2. What does it mean to enter the sanctuary in our current day (verse 17)?

3. What does it mean that our heart and flesh may fail (verse 26)?

4. How might Asaph's reflections in the psalm have led to his last statement, "I will tell of all your deeds" (verse 28)?

Connect to the Heart of Jesus

Everything changed when Asaph stepped into the sanctuary—the place where God's presence dwelt in the Old Testament (Exodus 25:8–9; Psalm 68:35).

As a Levitical musician appointed by King David (1 Chronicles 6:39; 25:1), **Asaph served at the Tent of Meeting,** the tabernacle David set up for the ark in Jerusalem—the movable dwelling place of God's presence. When Asaph entered the sanctuary, he stepped into both the physical and spiritual presence of God.

Centuries later, everything changed again.

John 1 tells us that Jesus "made his dwelling among us" (verse 14). The Greek word used here is σκηνόω *(skēnóō)*, meaning "to dwell" or "to tabernacle."[34] John is showing us that we no longer have to travel to a physical tabernacle—because Jesus became the tabernacle. God Himself came to dwell among us, and now, through His Spirit, He lives within us.

This truth became visibly real at the moment of Jesus' death. Matthew 27:51 says,

The curtain of the temple was torn
in two from top to bottom.

That curtain once separated the people from the holy of holies—the place where God's presence resided and where only the high priest could enter. When Jesus died, that barrier was forever removed. His sacrifice opened the way for direct access to God, to this incredible strength of our hearts that Asaph describes and desires more than anything on this earth (Psalm 73:26).

And yet, **how often do we rebuild barriers ourselves?**

We let shame, religiosity, or the belief that others are "closer" to God hold us back. But the torn curtain still stands as a reminder: Jesus already made the way. We have the same access Asaph longed for—only now, God's presence isn't limited to a place. It lives in us. What are we waiting for? The invitation to God's personal, constant presence through Jesus is the song Jesus continues to sing over our lives:

"Come to me . . ."

(MATTHEW 11:28)

---

34 *Strong's* Greek 4637, σκηνόω (skēnóō): to dwell, to tabernacle, to pitch a tent.

Apply & Take Action

1. How have I seen being in the presence of God change my life or perspective lately? What is something I need Him to change through His presence?

2. Is there something I desire more than His presence on this earth (verse 25)? How can I allow this psalm to shape me?

3. Who is far from God that is perishing without salvation (verse 27)? Who can I pray for today to come to know Him?

Pray and ask God to help you apply His truth to your life.

BIBLE BITES for PSALM 73: 18-28

1. The **shekinah glory** (God's visible presence) appeared as a cloud by day and a pillar of fire by night over the tabernacle (Exodus 40:34–38).

2. Asaph led worship alongside a man named Heman before God's presence (1 Chronicles 6:39; 25:1), not to be confused with the heroic He-Man action figure.

3. When Asaph says he was a "brute beast" (verse 22), the Hebrew phrase indicates a dumb or wild beast.

STUDY 19

Finding a Song in the Night

Psalm 77

KEY VERSE

I remembered my songs in the night.

(VERSE 6)

Pause . . . pray . . . and ask God for help in today's study.

Do you ever have difficulty with sleep? If you do, you are not alone. According to a survey by the American Academy of Sleep Medicine (AASM) carried out in May 2024, 36% of US adults reported having been diagnosed with a sleep-related disorder.[35] And in a separate AASM

35 American Academy of Sleep Medicine, *2024 Sleep Prioritization Survey: Sleep Disorder Diagnosis*, conducted by Atomik Research, fieldwork May 2024, https://aasm.org/wp-content/uploads/2024/09/sleep-prioritization-survey-2024-sleep-disorder-diagnosis.pdf.

survey conducted in March 2023, 53 percent of Americans indicated that they "always" or "often" have trouble staying asleep.[36] While a variety of causes may underlie such difficulties, data on anxiety suggest that many of us struggle with sleep because of it. And as it turns out, those in the ancient world were not immune to sleep difficulties either. We now turn to one of Asaph's psalms, where he invites us into a night—or perhaps nights—of sleeplessness. (Maybe we don't have to blame all of our sleep difficulties on our smartphones!) This psalm will bring comfort: We are not alone, God does care about our sleep, and surprisingly, we will learn that what might be keeping us awake at times is not just our anxiousness or worries—but God Himself.

Look Deeper

Open your Bible and read Psalm 77 at least once.

1. What does Asaph's approach to God tell us about Him?

2. What can we learn about the heart of mankind in these verses?

36 American Academy of Sleep Medicine, *2023 Sleep Prioritization Survey: Staying Asleep*, conducted by Atomik Research, fieldwork March 2023, https://aasm.org/wp-content/uploads/2023/06/sleep-prioritization-survey-2023-staying-asleep.pdf.

We ended our last study with Asaph beautifully declaring that God was his refuge (Psalm 73:28) and that there was nothing he desired more than God Himself (verses 25–26). Yet in this next psalm, we find Asaph struggling once again. Whether you find that comforting or discouraging, it reminds us of an essential truth: We never "arrive" spiritually on this earth. There are no spiritual superheroes free of mistakes. Even the faithful wrestle and return to God again and again.

The psalms show us this rhythm repeatedly—a continual returning, a continual crying out for help. As Asaph writes,

I cried out to God for help;
I cried out to God to hear me.
When I was in distress, I sought the Lord.

(PSALM 77:1–2)

Asaph doesn't tell us exactly what caused his distress, but perhaps that silence is an invitation—an opening for each of us to bring our own distress before the Lord.

He goes on to describe long, sleepless nights, saying that he stretched out his hands to God without comfort (verse 2). If there had been an "Ancient Israelite Academy of Sleep Medicine," Asaph might well have been one of its case studies!

But then comes a surprising realization. Asaph suggests that his sleeplessness wasn't caused only by anxiety or sorrow:

You kept my eyes from closing.

(PSALM 77:4)

I still remember the moment I paused on that phrase during study—the simple yet profound idea that God Himself may, at times, keep us awake.

Could it be that some nights of sleeplessness are interruptions—moments when God stirs our hearts, inviting us to seek Him more deeply?

Through Asaph's journey, we will learn that **there is a rest deeper than sleep**—a rest that comes only from God. And often, when we seek that kind of rest, true sleep follows naturally.

What Does the Scripture Mean?

1. Why does Asaph reflect on the "former days" (verse 5) in his distress? How do you think this led to his lamenting questions (verses 7–9)?

2. What were the practice(s) Asaph decided to turn to (verses 11–12)?

3. Why does Asaph recall the exodus story as a response to his questions in verses 7–9? What might these stories mean for his current distress?

4. How might the placement of "Selah" in this psalm (at the end of verses 3, 9, and 15 ESV) reveal a structure?

Connect to the Heart of Jesus

The author of Hebrews tells us that Jesus may have joined Asaph's practice of crying out to God—not only in the garden of Gethsemane, but throughout His earthly life:

During the days of Jesus' life on earth, he offered up prayers and petitions with fervent cries and tears to the one who could save him from death, and he was heard because of his reverent submission.

(HEBREWS 5:7)

Jesus' response to distress reveals both His humanity and His divinity. In His humanity, He cried out to the Father for help; in His divinity, He invited others to bring their distress to Him:

> *"Come to me, all you who are weary and burdened,*
> *and I will give you rest."*
>
> (MATTHEW 11:28)

Like Asaph, Jesus invites us to bring our weariness, our sleepless nights, and our questions about where God is—directly to Him. As we have seen over and over again in our study of the psalms, Jesus and the authors of the psalms show us that honest lament can coexist with deep faith. But Asaph does not stop with lament—he turns to *remembrance*. In the middle of his turmoil, he recalls God's faithfulness and mighty acts of salvation, saying, "I will remember the deeds of the LORD; yes, I will remember your miracles of long ago" (Psalm 77:11). This act of remembering becomes the turning point of his faith.

Whoa. Let's say that again in case we skimmed past it: **This act of remembering becomes the turning point of Asaph's faith.** This act is no little act.

No wonder that one of the most significant practices of the Christian faith handed down by Jesus is that of *remembrance*. On the night He was betrayed, Jesus took bread and said, "Do this in remembrance of me" (Luke 22:19). Just as Asaph found renewed faith by remembering God's past deliverance, we are called to remember Christ's ultimate act of salvation on the cross. In both, remembrance transforms distress into trust, helping our weary hearts find rest in God.

Apply & Take Action

1. When I have sleepless nights due to distress, **do I turn to God first?**

2. Are there honest questions I have been holding back from God, that could be encouraged by Asaph's model in verses 7–9?

3. What are some miracles or works of faithfulness I have seen in my life that I can have ready to remember in times of distress?

4. Who is someone in my life facing distress that needs the encouragement to remember what God has done in the past?

Pray and ask God to help you apply His truth to your life.

BIBLE BITES for PSALM 77

1. Though deeply personal, Asaph didn't mean for Psalm 77 to stay personal. The title instructs Jeduthun to **lead this psalm in music**.

2. Charles Spurgeon wrote that he understood Asaph in Psalm 77 because he had also experienced deep "soul depressions."[37]

3. Asaph may be describing rain, thunder, and lightning that was happening during the parting of the Red Sea (verses 17–18), which gives greater detail to the Exodus version.

37 David Guzik, "Psalm 77—the Troubled Heart Remembers God's Great Works," *Enduring Word Bible Commentary*, Enduring Word, accessed November 5, 2025, https://enduringword.com/bible-commentary/psalm-77.

STUDY 20

Arise, God: Our Champion of the Weak

Psalm 82

KEY VERSE

Defend the weak and the fatherless;
uphold the cause of the poor and the oppressed.

(VERSE 3)

Pause . . . pray . . . and ask God for help in today's study.

How would you answer if someone asked you, "Aside from God, what topic does the Bible address more than anything else?" Would it surprise you to learn that the most frequent subject is the poor? It certainly surprised me when I first learned that **the Bible speaks on the poor, widowed, and destitute more than three thousand times**. But it didn't just surprise me—it challenged me. It stirred something in me and invited me to align my heart more closely with the heart of God.

Today's psalm draws us into this theme—God's deep love and concern for the poor, the weak, the oppressed, and the fatherless. These are all people Scripture gathers under the banner of "the poor," those who are vulnerable and in need of refuge and care.

As we pray today, let's ask God to shape our hearts—to help us feel what He feels, to care about what He cares about. May our hearts break for what breaks His.

Look Deeper

Open your Bible and **read Psalm 82** at least once.

1. What does this psalmist teach us about God in these verses, both in His actions and character?

2. What types of people does the psalm mention, and what do we learn about mankind through this mention?

We continue our journey with Asaph, and in this psalm he takes on a fascinating role. **Asaph steps into the position of a preacher and teacher,** addressing the so-called gods—a term best understood as human judges (as Jesus later confirms in John 10:34).

But in an unexpected twist, Asaph turns the courtroom around: The judges themselves are now on trial.

Asaph charges them with a double failure—defending the wrong people (the wicked and unjust, verse 2) and failing to defend the right ones (the weak, fatherless, poor, and oppressed, verse 3). In doing so, he echoes a theme that runs throughout Scripture: God's deep concern for the vulnerable.

Asaph's words reflect the very heart of God, the same heartbeat we hear in Psalm 12:5:

"Because the poor are plundered and the needy groan,
I will now arise," says the LORD.

Just as God rises to defend the oppressed, Asaph lifts his voice to call out injustice and plead for righteousness. His psalm reminds us that true worship doesn't turn a blind eye to suffering—it reflects the compassion and justice of the God who says, "I will now arise" (verse 5).

And though Asaph finds the earthly judges worthy of being brought to trial, he reminds them of the great equalizer—death—to humble them.

Despite what man may do to the poor and oppressed, Asaph reminds us they are never forgotten, and God will defend them.

What Does the Scripture Mean?

1. What does it mean to "defend the unjust" (verse 2)?

2. What might Asaph mean when he says that "all the foundations of the earth are shaken" (verse 5)?

3. What does it mean for God to defend the poor and the needy, in ancient times and still today?

4. What does it mean that all the nations are God's inheritance (verse 8)? Why does Asaph finish with this statement?

Connect to the Heart of Jesus

Jesus made His love for Psalm 82 abundantly clear in the Gospel of John. In John 10, Jesus is in Jerusalem during the Feast of Dedication—which today is Hanukkah—and the leaders demand He tell them if He is the Christ: "If you are the Messiah, tell us plainly" (verse 24). After declaring, "I and the Father are one" (verse 30), the religious leaders pick up stones to stone Jesus for blasphemy, because they see exactly what He is doing—making Himself equal to God (verse 33).

It's at this moment, in John 10:34–36, that Jesus quotes Psalm 82:

Jesus answered them, "Is it not written in your Law,
'I have said you are "gods"'? If he called them 'gods,'
to whom the word of God came—and Scripture
cannot be set aside—what about the one whom the
Father set apart as his very own and sent into the world?
Why then do you accuse me of
blasphemy because I said, 'I am God's Son'?"

Jesus masterfully uses this passage to expose His accusers' hypocrisy and to reveal His identity. His reasoning is powerful. Jesus is essentially saying, if corrupt human judges can be called gods by Scripture because they bear God's delegated word, how much more rightful is it for Jesus, the One whom the Father has sanctified and sent into the world, to call Himself the Son of God? He appeals to their own Scriptures and reasoning. In essence Jesus is saying, "You know Psalm 82—how God rebukes those who misuse His authority, specifically to mistreat and oppress the marginalized. Now behold the One who perfectly wields it."

Then, in compassion, Jesus extends a final plea:

"Do not believe me unless I do the works of my Father. But if I do them, even though you do not believe me, believe the works, that you may know and understand that the Father is in me, and I in the Father."

(JOHN 10:37–38)

And again, the leaders try to seize Him (verse 39). **But even as stones are raised, Jesus overflows with mercy.** Jesus uses Psalm 82 for apologetics, but also to try to appeal to the hearts of those listening to believe in Him. Where Asaph spoke God's heart, Jesus embodied it—He is the righteous Judge who came to do what the human judges failed to do.

Apply & Take Action

1. Are there any ways in my life that I turn a blind eye to injustice? **How can I grow a deeper love for those facing injustice?**

2. Who are the weak and fatherless around me? How can I use the resources or opportunities I have been given to care for more of them?

3. What can I learn from the way Jesus used Psalm 82 to correct error and to extend grace?

4. Who can I share some of the truths I've learned from Psalm 82 with this week?

Pray and ask God to help you apply His truth to your life.

BIBLE BITES for PSALM 82

1. Psalm 82:1 uses the word *Elohim* twice but for very different reasons: first for the true God, and second for *gods*—the human judges. This is seen as **a poetic contrast between the judge and those judged.**

2. Early church father Augustine saw Psalm 82 as a foreshadowing of Jesus' coming—the moment when God Himself "arose" to judge the earth and restore righteousness through His Son.[38]

3. Ancient Near Eastern texts often describe councils of gods. Asaph uses this idea but reshapes it from a monotheistic—the one, true God—view.

38 Augustine, "Exposition on Psalm 82," New Advent, accessed March 24, 2026, www.newadvent .org/fathers/1801082.htm.

STUDY 21

Justice for God's Cherished

Psalm 83

KEY VERSE

Let them know that you, whose name is the LORD—
that you alone are the Most High over all the earth.

(VERSE 18)

Pause . . . pray . . . and ask God for help in today's study.

Today we step into what is known as an **imprecatory psalm,** written by our familiar friend Asaph. Imprecatory psalms are **psalms that invoke God's justice, curse, and judgment upon His enemies.** While a psalm like Psalm 83 might be harder to swallow than others, underneath the harsh language found within the imprecatory psalms are beautiful truths that can reveal more of the character of God. There are about fourteen major imprecatory psalms, with many other psalms comprising some imprecatory language. Before reading Psalm 83, consider this word from Got Questions Ministries on the imprecatory psalms:

> When studying the imprecatory psalms, it is important to note that these psalms were not written out of vindictiveness or a need for personal vengeance. Instead, they are prayers that keep God's justice, sovereignty, and protection in mind. God's people had suffered much at the hands of those who opposed them, including the Hittites, Amorites, Philistines, and Babylonians (the subject of Psalm 137). These groups were not only enemies of Israel, but they were also enemies of God; they were degenerate and ruthless conquerors who had repeatedly tried and failed to destroy the Lord's chosen people. In writing the imprecatory psalms, the authors sought vindication on God's behalf as much as they sought their own.[39]

Look Deeper

Open your Bible and read Psalm 83 at least once.

1. What does the psalm tell us about God?

39 "What Are the Imprecatory Psalms?" GotQuestions, accessed March 24, 2026, www.gotquestions.org/imprecatory-psalms.html.

2. What do the author's words tell us about His heart and the reflection on mankind in general?

Good old Asaph—our honest, unfiltered friend. Psalm 83 opens with another heart-wrenching plea: "O God, do not remain silent." Once again, Asaph isn't afraid to say what many of us feel but might hesitate to admit out loud. If a church leader spoke this way today, some might gasp—but for the rest of us, it's strangely comforting. It reminds us we're not alone when God's silence feels heavy.

Asaph's cry isn't coming from a place of casual frustration. God's people are surrounded by enemies, and he makes it clear these foes aren't simply opposed to Israel—they're opposed to God Himself. Asaph describes them as rising up against "those you cherish" (verse 3). The Hebrew carries rich layers of meaning: The ESV and CSB translate it as "your treasured ones," while the King James uses "thy hidden ones." Each translation paints the same picture—God's people are precious, protected, deeply loved. And **Asaph appeals to God on the basis of that love.**

What makes the situation even more sobering is that this isn't a single enemy. Asaph lists ten nations conspiring together, forming a unified alliance against God's people—and therefore against God. The weight of the threat matches the weight of Asaph's plea: "God, speak. Act. Don't stay silent now."

And then Asaph launches into his imprecatory pleadings, with not just general curses but specific ones, culminating in his plea to God to "terrify them with [His] storm" (verse 15). But as we go deeper into the psalm, we'll begin to see the underlying grace of God—and even a surprising grace reflected in Asaph himself—beneath these cries for judgment.

What Does the Scripture Mean?

1. What might it have meant if Israel's name had been "remembered no more" (verse 4)?

2. The word *selah*—most likely meaning to pause or ponder—follows verses 1–8 (ESV). Why do you think Asaph wanted the reader (including us) to pause here and ponder the words?

3. How did God deal with Midian (verse 9)? (Skim over Judges 6–8 if you have time, or find a reliable summary.)

4. What does the surprising statement in verse 16 reveal about Asaph's ultimate heart for the reason he calls down hardship upon the opposing nations?

5. How do we reconcile Asaph's desire in verses 16 and 18 with his other desire that "they perish in disgrace" (verse 17)?

Connect to the Heart of Jesus

Would you be surprised to know that Jesus—who teaches us to love and pray for our enemies—quoted some of the imprecatory psalms? For instance, John tells us that Jesus referenced Psalm 69:4 (ESV) in the upper room, noting how the Jews "hated me without a cause" (John 15:25 ESV). Later, when Jesus is on the cross, John records: "Knowing that everything had now been finished, and so that Scripture would be fulfilled, Jesus said, 'I am thirsty.' A jar of wine vinegar was there, so they soaked a sponge in it, put the sponge on a stalk of the hyssop plant, and lifted it to Jesus' lips" (John 19:28–29). John makes it clear that this moment fulfilled Psalm 69:21: "They put gall in my food and gave me vinegar for my thirst." In other words, Jesus didn't just love Psalm 69; He fulfilled it.

Like Psalm 69, Psalm 83 is another imprecatory psalm inspired by the Holy Spirit and beloved by Jesus. But the fulfillment goes even deeper. Jesus became the very curse that the psalmists called upon: "Christ redeemed us from the curse of the law by becoming a curse for us" (Galatians 3:13). This flips the script—because it shows that all of us, not just the enemies of Israel, deserved a curse for our sin. All of us were enemies of God. Yet, while we were still enemies, we were reconciled to Him through the death of His Son: "For if, while we were God's enemies, we were reconciled to him through the death of his Son, how much more, having been reconciled, shall we be saved through his life!" (Romans 5:10).

On a personal note, as I study this alongside you, I am amazed at the deeper fulfillment of the imprecatory psalms in Jesus. I hope this reflection blows your mind and touches your heart as it has mine. As Greg Morse writes in his article "'Oh Slay the Wicked': How Christians Sing Curses":

> Christ became a cursed one, a doomed and condemned man—why? For us. The bread, broken—for you. The wine, poured out—for you. The judgment drank to the bottom—for you. The history of all curses for every human on the planet ends here, at the cross, or in hell. Nowhere else.[40]

Indeed, we can rest in the fulfillment of the imprecatory psalms in Jesus, knowing that what once expressed **the psalmists' cries for justice and vengeance were perfectly answered and completed in Him,** for the salvation of all who believe.

---

40 Greg Morse, "'Oh Slay the Wicked': How Christians Sing Curses," Desiring God, September 6, 2023, www.desiringgod.org/articles/oh-slay-the-wicked.

Apply & Take Action

1. Have I or do I feel like God is or has been silent in my life? How can this psalm encourage me when God feels silent?

2. What are things I feel righteous anger over? How might I express that to God today?

3. How can Asaph's plea that his enemies seek and know God's name (verses 16, 18) encourage me to pray for my enemies or those I struggle with loving today?

4. Who in my life needs to be reconciled to God through Jesus? How can I pray for or reach out to them this week?

Pray and ask God to help you apply His truth to your life.

BIBLE BITES for PSALM 83

1. The Moabites and Ammonites were descendants of Lot, Abraham's nephew, who became enemies at various times to Israel (verse 8).

2. Some people see Psalm 83 as a prophecy of other nations attacking Jews and also as a prophecy of a future war on Israel.

3. Many commentators are surprised that Egypt was left out of the list of nations in Psalm 83, as it was a major player in the ancient world and rose up against Israel.

STUDY 22

Where Our Souls Find Home

Psalm 84

KEY VERSE

Better is one day in your courts than a thousand elsewhere.

(VERSE 10)

Pause . . . pray . . . and ask God for help in today's study.

We're stepping into a psalm written by the Sons of Korah, and it's worth pausing to hear Charles Spurgeon's words about this psalm, which he famously called "The Pearl of Psalms." He wrote:

If the twenty-third be the most popular, the one-hundred-and-third the most joyful, the one-hundred-and-nineteenth the most deeply experimental, the fifty-first the most plaintive, this is one of the most sweet of the Psalms of peace.[41]

Following Spurgeon's metaphor, just as pearls are found only by diving beneath the surface where the mollusks dwell, we, too, must be willing to go deep into this psalm if we want to uncover its beauty.

Look Deeper

Open your Bible and read Psalm 84 at least once.

1. What do the author's pleas and descriptions of God reveal about God's character?

2. What do you learn about people from this psalm?

Psalm 84 centers on the journey to Jerusalem—the place where God's people gathered around the temple, or before that, the tabernacle. The psalmist begins

41 Charles Spurgeon, "Psalm 84," Blue Letter Bible, accessed November 18, 2025, www.blueletterbible.org/Comm/spurgeon_charles/tod/ps084.cfm.

by expressing this aching, almost physical longing for the "dwelling place" of God (verse 1). Yes, God's presence was connected to a physical structure, but the author makes it unmistakably clear: He isn't craving a building. His heart is longing for God Himself: "My heart and my flesh cry out for the living God" (verse 2).

Out of that longing, he notices something small but profound—whether literally or symbolically—that even the birds have made their homes near God's altar, building nests and raising their young (verse 3). Birds only nest where they're safe and unbothered. I can attest to that personally, as my husband and I have an annual (funny) war regarding the birds that want to nest in our pergola in our backyard. He does everything to disrupt and disturb their nesting, and I protect it as much as I can so we get baby birds in our yard. **The scene of birds nesting near the altar of God shows a subtle but stunning picture of how secure, welcomed, and cared for we are in God's presence.**

The psalmist's reflections on God's house, paired with his words "Blessed are those who dwell in your house" (verse 4), reveal something deeper: Our safest home—our truest home—is not a place at all but the presence of God. And it's from that place of belonging that he continues, "Blessed are those whose strength is in you, whose hearts are set on pilgrimage" (verse 5). Happy, fulfilled, deeply rooted are those who draw their strength from God rather than anything else—and who set their hearts on journeying with Him and toward Him.

The psalmist is so overwhelmed by the goodness of God's presence that he says one day with God is better than a thousand anywhere else. And as if that isn't bold enough, he goes further: He'd rather hold the lowest job in God's house—a simple doorkeeper—than enjoy comfort or prosperity "in the tents of the wicked" (verse 10). In other words: I'd rather be close to God in the lowest place than far from Him in the highest one.

Wouldn't it be amazing if that was our one desire!

If we carried even a fraction of the desire this psalmist expresses, it would transform the way we pursue God.

What Does the Scripture Mean?

1. What does it mean to be someone who yearns and even faints for God (verse 2)? What does that look like in practice?

2. The meaning of Valley of Baka (verse 6) is uncertain but is understood to most likely mean the Valley of Weeping. What does it mean that one who has their strength in God is able to walk through a valley or season of weeping and make it "a place of springs" (verse 6)?

3. What does it mean that the one journeying toward God goes "from strength to strength" (verse 7)?

4. In light of difficulties in life, what does verse 11 mean: "No good thing does he withhold from those whose walk is blameless"?

Connect to the Heart of Jesus

While the psalmist longed to dwell in the temple, Jesus spoke words that would change everything: "Destroy this temple, and in three days I will raise it up" (John 2:19 ESV)—a statement referring, of course, to His own body (John 2:21). Indeed, His body—the true temple—was destroyed and then raised on the third day. The longing expressed in Psalm 84—to dwell continually in God's presence within His temple—was ultimately fulfilled in Jesus. **He became the meeting place of God and humanity.** And with the gift of His Spirit, we no longer journey to and from the temple; God's presence now dwells with us constantly.

We often take for granted what the psalmist cried out for. I once had a friend point out how easy it is to look back at the miracles of the Old Testament and think, *Wouldn't my faith be so much stronger if I had seen God work in those ways?* But the truth is, we have something even greater: the living God residing within us, never leaving. The friend went on to remind me that **we literally have what the psalmists longed for!**

The New Testament expands on this reality: Every believer is a living stone in this new spiritual temple (1 Corinthians 3:16; Ephesians 2:22; 1 Peter 2:4–5), and together, as the church, we are God's dwelling place on earth. Sadly, we live in a day when gathering as the body of Christ is often taken lightly—people drift between churches, casually and frequently skip gatherings, or claim that all they need is God personally. But God designed His people to be interconnected. Each believer is a part of the body, and **we are meant to gather, encourage, and serve one another.** Together, we reflect the fullness of Christ in ways we cannot do alone. Being present with God's people is not optional; it is part of the life God created for us, to reflect the living temple of God.

Apply & Take Action

1. Am I experiencing the presence of God as better than anything else in this life (verse 10)? If not, what do I think is getting in the way?

2. How might God be calling me to further build up the body of Christ as part of the spiritual temple through Christ?

3. In what areas of my life am I finding it hard to trust God (verse 12)? What untrue thoughts or assumptions might be getting in the way of that trust?

4. How might God be speaking to me through this psalm about longing for or sitting in His presence more? Who in my life needs to be encouraged by spending more time in His presence?

Pray and ask God to help you apply His truth to your life.

BIBLE BITES for PSALM 84

1) Psalm 84 has been incredibly popular in hymns and songs, including "Better Is One Day" by Matt Redman.

2) Psalm 84 is considered one of the "Zion" psalms, which have been known in Jewish tradition as focusing on the dwelling place of God.[42]

42 J. Edwin Orr, "Prayer and Revival," J. Edwin Orr (website), accessed November 19, 2025, https://jedwinorr.com/resources/articles/prayandrevival.pdf.

STUDY 23

Revive Our Hearts

Psalm 85

KEY VERSE

Will you not revive us again, that your people may rejoice in you?

(VERSE 6)

Pause . . . pray . . . and ask God for help in today's study.

Today we're talking about revival—not the huge outdoor meetings or packed stadiums we usually picture, but a revival of the heart. This kind of renewal starts small, through prayer and repentance. Sure, revival can show up in big, visible ways, but it always begins inside us, when we come before God honestly and earnestly.

Dr. A. T. Pierson, a well-known pastor and evangelist, put it this way: "There has never been a spiritual awakening in any country or locality that did not begin in united prayer."[43] In other words, history has no record of revival that didn't start on its knees.

Whether it's a large-scale movement or a quiet renewal in our own hearts after feeling distant or distracted from God, Psalm 85 reminds us—just like Pierson said—it all begins in prayer.

Look Deeper

Open your Bible and **read Psalm 85** at least once.

1. What attribute(s) about God in this passage stand(s) out to you most?

2. What do the author's prayers teach you about a relationship with God?

---

43 Marshall Segal, "Restore Our Joy in You: A Prayer for God-Centered Revival," Desiring God, November 13, 2024, www.desiringgod.org/messages/restore-our-joy-in-you.

Like Psalm 84, Psalm 85 is attributed to the Sons of Korah and was written for the director of music. The psalm opens with a heartfelt reminder of God's past kindness—how He once showed favor to His people and wiped away their sins. That memory isn't just nostalgia; it becomes the launching point for the next plea, where the writer openly admits that they've felt the weight of God's displeasure and desperately need His forgiveness again (verses 4–5).

Forgive the moment of humor, but I picture this exchange like a kid approaching a parent: "Yes, we messed up. Yes, you're upset. But, hey—remember how you forgave our siblings? Could you forgive us, too?" It's a bit funny, but it also captures something real: our boldness in coming to God and His steady willingness to show mercy.

Then comes the cry that rises from the heart of the psalm: "Will you not revive us again, that your people may rejoice in you?" (verse 6). The next verse adds a crucial reminder of where revival actually comes from: "Show us your unfailing love, LORD, and grant us your salvation" (verse 7). Revival isn't something we manufacture—it's something God pours out. It springs from His loyal love and His saving power, not our performance or doing.

The closing section almost feels like it was written after experiencing that revival firsthand because it reads like a grateful response to God's renewing work. The writer makes a personal commitment: "I will listen to what God the LORD says" (verse 8). The Hebrew word for "listen" here is *shāma*,[44] a word that means far more than just hearing sounds. The word indicates attentive listening that leads to obedience. In other words, true revival doesn't just make people hear God's words—it stirs a desire to respond, to follow, to obey.

Revived people don't just listen to God. Revived people lean in and let His voice reshape their lives.

---

44 James Strong, *The Exhaustive Concordance of the Bible* (Abingdon Press, 1890), s.v. "H8085."

What Does the Scripture Mean?

1. What might the beginning of the psalm suggest about one's approach to coming to God when they feel distant?

2. What does it mean for God to "set aside" His wrath (verse 3)? What is the wrath of God, and does it differ from anger?

3. **What is the relationship between God's anger and His love** in this psalm? How does the psalm hold both together without contradiction?

4. How does the promise of peace in verse 8 relate to the call for God's people not to return to folly? What kind of peace is described?

5. What does the author mean with the metaphors "love and faithfulness meet together" and "righteousness and peace kiss each other" (verse 10)?

Connect to the Heart of Jesus

While the Sons of Korah looked back on all that God had done for His people—how He showed favor to their land, restored the fortunes of Jacob, and, most remarkably, forgave the iniquity of His people (verses 1–2)—we look back on something even greater: what God has done for us through Jesus. In other words, our "looking back" is richer and more complete.

On a personal note, every Christmas season I pray David's words from Psalm 51:12, "Restore to me the joy of your salvation." Like the cry of Psalm 85, I long for a renewed heart—for God to revive me and restore the joy of my salvation as I remember all that Jesus has accomplished. We now have far more to rest upon as we plead, "Restore us again" (verse 4) and "revive us again" (verse 6).

And as we look to the heart of Jesus, who poured out His life for us, **we see at the cross the perfect meeting of love and faithfulness,** the most beautiful "kiss" of righteousness and peace (verse 10). Marshall Segal says it beautifully:

> Righteousness and peace meet in Jesus. They come together, like two massive beams, at the cross. And they don't just meet. They don't just reluctantly agree to work together for a couple of years—no, they kiss. There's no tension or distance between these two, not when they meet in this God, in this gospel. They kiss, for all who believe, beneath the broken body and poured out blood of Jesus. Because of Jesus, God is not angry with you anymore. He stands ready to forgive you, to revive you, and to fill your heart to bursting with joy, all for his glory.[45]

Jesus' life, death, and resurrection sing the good news of Psalm 85: "The LORD will indeed give what is good" (verse 12).

Apply & Take Action

1. Which part of Psalm 85 is most relatable in my own spiritual life right now—desperation, listening, hope, or renewal? Why?

---

45 Marshall Segal, "Restore Our Joy in You: A Prayer for God-Centered Revival," Desiring God, November 13, 2024, https://www.desiringgod.org/messages/restore-our-joy-in-you.

2. What is my experience of revival, whether personally or on a large scale? How do I need my heart more revived today?

3. Is there any sin I need to repent of as I look to God for revival? What (if anything) might be standing in the way of my renewal or revival?

4. What is something that God is prompting me to respond to with verse 8: “I will listen to [obey] what God the LORD says”?

Pray and ask God to help you apply His truth to your life.

BIBLE BITES for PSALM 85

1. The Hebrew word for "turn back," *shuv* (בוּשׁ)[46], is used four times in this psalm—verses 1, 3, 4, and 6—a central theme in this passage.

2. The words and phrases "steadfast love" (ESV), "faithfulness," and "righteousness" to describe God echo Exodus 34:6–7, the Old Testament's most prolific description of God.

3. The phrase "covered all their sin" (verse 2) is one of the strongest in the Bible to describe salvation, and it's no wonder it is followed by "Selah" (ESV).

46 Hebrew Word Lessons, "Shuv: Return, Restore, Turn Back," https://hebrewwordlessons.com/2021/05/30/shuv-return-restore-turn-back/.

STUDY 24

When We Can't Find the Light

Psalm 88

KEY VERSE

Darkness is my closest friend.

(VERSE 18)

Pause . . . pray . . . and ask God for help in today's study.

Today we're diving into a psalm that ends with a line you don't expect to find in the Bible: "Darkness is my closest friend" (verse 18). (Anyone else singing the song lyric from Simon and Garfunkel's "The Sound of Silence" in their head, *Hello darkness my old friend . . .*?) **There's no neat conclusion to this psalm.** No last-minute turnaround where the writer proclaims, "But I still trust God." It just . . . ends. Heavy. Unresolved.

But there's something strangely beautiful about that.

And on a personal note, the timing couldn't have been more fitting. I wrote this study on a day when the sky outside was dark and heavy, the week had been rough, and I was struggling to see any kind of light in a few areas of my life. Digging deep into this psalm ended up being oddly comforting. It doesn't force a smile or pretend everything is fine—and that felt cathartic.

My hope is that this psalm reminds us of something important: **The Bible is beautiful not just when it offers answers, but also when it sits with us in the moments when things are very much not okay.**

Look Deeper

Open your Bible and **read Psalm 88** at least once.

1. What do you learn about the author, Heman the Ezrahite, from 1 Chronicles 6:33 and 25:4–6?

2. How does the author's first statement, "LORD, you are the God who saves me" (verse 1), align or not to seem to align with the rest of the psalm? What does this tell us about God and mankind?

3. What are some of the specific struggles the author is faced with?

There's something pretty striking about the fact that this is the only psalm written by Heman the Ezrahite, a respected leader among God's people. (Hopefully you checked out his history in the questions above!) If you only get one shot at writing a psalm, you might expect it to be filled with gratitude, blessing, or some kind of spiritual highlight reel. But Heman goes in the complete opposite direction. His one contribution is brutally honest. He basically says, "Everything is not okay." And that raw honesty is exactly why his words matter.

He opens with the only real spark of hope in the entire psalm—he reminds himself that God has saved him (verse 1). Thank goodness for that tiny glimmer, because the rest of what he shares is a tough swallow.

Heman is dealing with one of the deepest kinds of pain: being abandoned and rejected by his friends (verses 8, 18). Can you or have you ever been able to relate to this? But even heavier than that, he feels the weight of God's wrath (verses 7, 16). He feels forgotten and rejected by God Himself (verse 14). And as if that weren't enough, he reveals that this isn't a new struggle—he's been suffering like this since he was young (verse 15).

Throughout the entire psalm, Heman keeps crying out, again and again, with no resolution in sight. But maybe that's the point. Maybe this psalm is showing us that biblical "resolution" isn't always about everything getting fixed. Sometimes the hope is actually in the conversation—in continuing to show up, to speak, to wrestle with God even when nothing feels resolved.

What Does the Scripture Mean?

1. The Old Testament believers had a limited understanding of death. What does verse 5 reveal about Heman's understanding of death? Briefly look at 2 Timothy 1:10. How did Jesus bring more understanding to death?

2. What does Psalm 88:6–8 reveal about Heman's understanding of where affliction comes from? How is this connected to a theological understanding of suffering?

3. Though it's filled with grief language and struggle, what does this psalm mean for someone in relationship with God?

4. On the surface, verse 1 can appear as the only hopeful place in the psalm. But what aspects of this psalm might speak to hope, faith, and light?

Connect to the Heart of Jesus

In one of only three places in the entire Bible where the strongest Greek word for depression or distress is used—*ademoneo*—it describes Jesus as He enters the garden of Gethsemane, praying in agony:

"My soul is overwhelmed with sorrow to the point of death."

(MARK 14:34)

Yes, Jesus knew the physical torture and death ahead of Him. But notice this: When He finally cried out on the cross, His words weren't about the physical pain at all. They were about something far deeper—the emotional and spiritual agony of feeling abandoned:

"My God, my God, why have you forsaken me?"

(MATTHEW 27:46)

And we learned that Jesus wasn't the first to pray from that place. Long before, in Psalm 88, Heman pours out a raw, unfiltered cry of emotional darkness—so heavy it practically echoes with despair. Charles Spurgeon captured this reality well:

> The mind can descend far lower than the body, for in it there are bottomless pits. The flesh can bear only a certain number of wounds . . . but the soul can bleed in ten thousand ways, and die over and over again each hour.[47]

We've probably all experienced the depths of emotional suffering in some capacity. For some, it's been a diagnosed depression; for others, it's the quieter aches of discouragement, loss, or loneliness. But one experience seems almost universal: feeling forsaken—by God, by people, or by the life we thought we'd have. Some of us have said it out loud, and some of us would never dare. But in Psalm 88, God gives us a surprising gift: permission to pray even the darkest prayers. **Because even though the psalm ends without a tidy resolution, it's still an act of faith.** Heman keeps bringing his pain to God, broken as it is. And then Jesus takes this even further. His cry of forsakenness wasn't confusion or shock. Earlier in the crucifixion story Scripture says:

Then Jesus, knowing all that would happen to him . . .

(JOHN 18:4 ESV)

He knew what He was walking into. **He stepped into the full weight of human anguish—spiritual, emotional, and physical.** And the forsakenness He felt was real. He bore our guilt, our judgment, our separation. The wrath meant for us was placed on Him, so we would never be forsaken, and so that we would never have to stand alone under the full weight of our sin. Jesus entered

---

47 Zack Eswine, *Spurgeon's Sorrows: Realistic Hope for Those Who Suffer from Depression* (Christian Focus Publications, 2014), 16.

the deepest darkness so that when we face our own shadows—whether mild sorrow or overwhelming despair—we can know this for certain: We are not alone, and we are not abandoned.

Apply & Take Action

1. Has there been a time when I have felt "overwhelmed with troubles" (verse 3)? How did I respond or seek comfort?

2. The psalmist continued to pray even while feeling like his prayers weren't answered. What does or what can encourage me to pray even when I feel my prayers are unanswered?

3. How might Psalm 88 help shape or transform my approach to others' sufferings?

4. In what ways am I, or can I be, a safe person for others to share with me in as raw of a way as Heman did?

Pray and ask God to help you apply His truth to your life.

BIBLE BITES for PSALM 88

1. Psalm 88 literally ends in darkness, since the Hebrew text has the word "darkness" at the end.

2. Heman was listed as one of the wisest men of the Bible (1 Kings 4:31).

3. Though Heman feels forgotten, he continues to use the personal name for God throughout Psalm 88.

STUDY 25

Fleeing Days, but a Faithful God

Psalm 90

KEY VERSE

Satisfy us in the morning with your unfailing love,
that we may sing for joy and be glad all our days.

(VERSE 14)

Pause . . . pray . . . and ask God for help in today's study.

I'll never forget reading Psalm 90 a couple of days after watching a New Year's Eve celebration, where a famous singer sang John Lennon's song, "Imagine," the first words being:

Imagine there's no heaven
It's easy if you try
No hell below us

Above us, only sky
Imagine all the people
Livin' for today[48]

In other words, how wonderful if all we have is today! Or . . . is it? Moses, the author of Psalm 90, tells us a different story. Like the words of Ecclesiastes—an honest and sobering reminder that our years are short—Moses will speak true wisdom regarding our days. And while we might nod our head that John Lennon's view of our days and lives misses the mark, do we truly live like our days matter for eternity? For those of us on the younger side, it might be hard to live in the reality that our days are short. But Psalm 90 invites us—maybe even pushes us—in a better direction. It calls us to walk in the reality of and **see our short lives through the lens of God's eternal faithfulness,** and to live with a wisdom that lasts longer than just "today."

Look Deeper

Open your Bible and **read Psalm 90** at least once.

1. What stands out to you about the way Moses speaks to and describes God?

48 John Lennon, "Imagine," track 1 on *Imagine* (Apple Records, 1971).

2. What does this tell you about both God and man?

Psalm 90 holds a unique place in Scripture as the only psalm explicitly attributed to Moses and as the first psalm in Book IV. Moses, born to Hebrew slaves in Egypt, rose to become the leader through whom God delivered His people from bondage. He guided Israel through the wilderness, instituted God's laws, and bore the heavy responsibility of shepherding God's covenant people. Deuteronomy 34:7 tells us that Moses died at one hundred twenty years old, "yet his eyes were not weak nor his strength gone." Throughout his long life, Moses witnessed—and led—God's people through countless moments of triumph and failure, joy and sorrow. He experienced the cycle of births and deaths, the weight of leadership, and the frailty of human life. It is fitting, then, that Psalm 90 opens with a meditation on the Lord's presence "throughout all generations" (verse 1).

Commentators debate when this psalm was composed, but I think we will find it suggests it comes from a man who has lived long enough to reflect deeply on the fleeting nature of life. In verses 3–6, Moses portrays human frailty through vivid metaphors, emphasizing God's sovereign control over life and death: He is the one who turns "people back to dust" (verse 3). This reflection naturally gives rise to humility. When one considers life's brevity—from dust to dust—human pride fades, replaced by a sober awareness of our dependence on God.

The psalm moves from humility to a contemplation of God's righteous judgment. In verses 7–11, Moses acknowledges God's wrath, a reality he himself had experienced firsthand. One might recall the episode of the golden calf: While

Moses was receiving the Ten Commandments on Mount Sinai, the people below had turned to idolatry. God's anger flared: "Now therefore let me alone, that my wrath may burn hot against them and I may consume them" (Exodus 32:10 ESV). Yet Moses interceded: "Turn from your fierce anger; relent and do not bring disaster on your people" (verse 12). Remarkably, God relented (verse 14). Moments like this likely shaped Moses' reflections in Psalm 90.

Against this backdrop, Moses contemplates life's brevity:

The years of our life are seventy, or even by reason of strength eighty;
yet their span is but toil and trouble; they are soon gone, and we fly away.

(PSALM 90:10 ESV)

Out of this awareness, he prays for wisdom: "Teach us to number our days, that we may gain a heart of wisdom" (verse 12). **Moses' understanding of wisdom is profoundly countercultural.** Life is not simply about living in the moment or indulging in pleasures, as John Lennon and other modern thinkers might suggest. Instead, recognizing the fleeting nature of our days calls for intentionality, reflection, and mindful dependence on God. As we study more, we will see what Moses teaches us about living in intentionality.

What Does the Scripture Mean?

1. What does verse 4 mean in relation to God's perspective of time? How does this compare to our view of time?

2. What does Moses' metaphor of "the new grass of the morning" mean (verse 5)?

3. Reflect on verses 10 and 15. How does Moses' perspective suggest he experienced more hardship than ease in his life? What insights does this give us about the balance of how we struggle in life, both for Moses and us today?

4. What specific wisdom can we gain by numbering our days (verse 12)?

5. How does the joy and gladness for life expressed and asked for in verse 14 contrast with what John Lennon's song and other worldly perspectives focus on?

6. Why does Moses end with a prayer to "establish the work of our hands" (verse 17)? How might numbering our days lead to a prayer like that?

Connect to the Heart of Jesus

As God Himself, **no one understood the fragility and brevity of human life more fully than Jesus,** a truth reflected in Psalm 90. He is the creator of all things (Colossians 1:16), yet He humbled Himself to live as one of us—subject to human limitations, the fleeting nature of our days, and even death itself. In His teachings, Jesus consistently invited His followers to reflect both on the brevity of earthly life and the eternal destiny of the soul. In other words, life on earth is short, but eternity is forever.

For example, in Matthew 6:19–34, Jesus contrasts earthly treasures with heavenly treasures, reminding us not to worry about tomorrow and to focus on the life to come more than our present life. In Luke 16:19–31, Jesus tells us a parable of a rich man whom God calls a fool for storing up and hoarding his wealth, and who dies unexpectedly, showing the brevity of a life on earth. And Jesus also calls us to look beyond the brevity of life and be ready and waiting for His return. In Matthew 24:42–44, He urges vigilance. The brevity and unpredictability of life demand spiritual preparedness for the coming of Jesus.

And yet with all the warnings of His coming while many of us are not prepared and His warnings about the fleeting nature of life, Paul reveals a beautiful truth about the timing of the Lord:

The Lord is not slow in keeping his promise, as some understand slowness. Instead he is patient with you, not wanting anyone to perish, but everyone to come to repentance.

(2 PETER 3:9)

Isn't this great news? Even in the midst of life's fleeting days, **God extends mercy and patience toward us and toward those who do not yet know Him.** Perhaps, like Moses in Psalm 90, we sometimes feel that the difficult days outweigh the good (verses 10, 15) and long for Christ's return. Yet God's "slowness" is not delay—it is love.

Jesus also calls us to make the most of our fleeting time. In the Great Commission (Matthew 28:18–20), He urges His followers not only to count their days, as Moses prayed, but to make their days count for the kingdom of God. Psalm 90 concludes with a prayer that can serve as both a reflection and a rallying cry for our mission:

May the favor of the Lord our God rest on us; establish the work of our hands for us—yes, establish the work of our hands.

(VERSE 17)

Whatever our calling—whether as career professionals, stay-at-home parents, married or single, young or old—God invites us to live intentionally, **making our lives a testimony that points to Jesus and His return.** May He establish the work of our hands and hearts, so that even in the brevity of life, our days point to Jesus.

Apply & Take Action

1. Do I have any "secret sins" that need to be brought to the light (verse 8)? If so, why don't I confess and bring them into the light of God's presence?

2. Can I relate to Moses' sentiment that he has seen more hard days than good? How does this psalm give me hope or comfort in my bad days?

3. What work has God called me to? How am I living or how can I live in light of the brevity of life and eternity through my work?

4. Who is someone in my life that seems to be living more for the here-and-now versus eternity? How can I encourage them this week?

Pray and ask God to help you apply His truth to your life.

BIBLE BITES for PSALM 90

1. With Moses as the author, Psalm 90 would be the oldest psalm written.

2. Some commentators suggest Moses might have written this psalm after the deaths of Aaron and Miriam and Moses' own sin in Numbers 20.

3. Though Moses' estimate of people living seventy to eighty years is relevant for today, **the oldest person to live in the Bible was Methuselah at 969 years** (Genesis 5:25–27).

STUDY 26

Under His Wings of Refuge

Psalm 91

KEY VERSE

Under his wings you will find refuge;
his faithfulness will be your shield and rampart.

(VERSE 4)

Pause . . . pray . . . and ask God for help in today's study.

Psalm 91 is one of the more familiar psalms in the Bible, but if there's one thing I hope you're discovering, it's that we can study a passage of Scripture again and again and still uncover new treasures each time. I hope you're finding that to be true with whichever psalms are familiar to you.

About five years ago, I started what I call a weekend psalm practice—simply meaning that every weekend, I spend time studying a different psalm. During the weekdays, I usually work through a different book of the Bible, but on weekends, it's all about the psalms.

As I've been writing this Bible study—and even revisiting psalms I've studied before, like Psalm 91—I keep being blown away. I can't tell you how many times my family has had to endure me saying at the end of a writing day, "You won't believe what I learned today in the psalms!" (Pray for them—they'll be hearing that a lot more!)

The Bible is full of treasures, and the psalms are a perfect example: familiar, yet endlessly rich, inviting us to dig deeper every single time we open them. So, let's dig into one of the few places in Scripture where God uses beautiful bird imagery to describe Himself—Psalm 91.

Look Deeper

Open your Bible and **read Psalm 91** at least once.

1. What are some of the attributes or actions of God that stand out to you from this psalm?

2. How is the person described who makes God their refuge, fortress, and place of trust? What does Psalm 91 reveal about that person's character or attitude?

The great and late preacher Charles Spurgeon argued of Psalm 91, "In the whole collection there is not a more cheering psalm, its tone is elevated and sustained throughout, faith is at its best, and speaks nobly," and he continues that this psalm "is a heavenly medicine against plague and pest."[49] Whether we agree with Spurgeon's assertion, it would be hard to deny that this psalm is meant to give comfort in the most difficult, dangerous, and darkest of circumstances, but also in the everyday challenges.

The author of Psalm 91, whose identity is unknown, begins by describing the one who "dwells in the shelter of the Most High." The Hebrew word for "dwells," (בַָשְׁי, *yā·sab*),[50] can also mean "to remain, sit, abide, or live"—suggesting a continuous, intentional presence. This reminds us that the rest described in the following phrase, "in the shadow of the Almighty" (verse 1), is not something we gain through a quick stop at a spiritual drive-through or by simply checking a box during a brief morning Bible study. (Though we are hoping through these twenty minutes, that's where it begins!) True refuge in God requires ongoing, abiding trust and intentional time with Him, a deep and sustained intimacy rather than a fleeting encounter. The author describes how this abiding led to trust:

---

49 Charles H. Spurgeon, "Treasury of David: Psalm 91," Blue Letter Bible, accessed November 7, 2025, https://www.blueletterbible.org/Comm/spurgeon_charles/tod/ps091.cfm.

50 James Strong, Strong's Exhaustive Concordance of the Bible, entry H3427, "yā·sab," Hebrew Lexicon, Blue Letter Bible, accessed November 7, 2025, for Psalm 91:1–2, https://www.blueletterbible.org/lexicon/h3427/kjv/wlc/0-1/.

I will say of the Lord, "He is my refuge and my fortress, my God, in whom I trust."

(VERSE 2)

Trust wasn't something that fell in the author's lap; it resulted from remaining in God's presence.

The psalmist continues with a series of assurances beginning with the statement, "Surely he will save you . . ." This is followed by a long list of dangers—both physical and spiritual—from which the one who dwells with the Lord will find protection. Later, the psalm reinforces this promise:

No harm will overtake you, no disaster will come near your tent.

(VERSE 10)

At first glance, this promise can be puzzling. **If God assures protection, why do the faithful still face trials,** as Asaph wrestled with in Psalm 73? Many of us reading this psalm may be walking through significant hardships right now, so what does this mean for us?

Got Questions Ministries offers helpful insight:

Psalm 91 does not provide immunity from life's threats. It does not promise God's protection from danger and trouble; it offers the promise of God's protection amid hardship and peril.[51]

---

51 "What Does It Mean to Dwell in the 'Shadow of the Almighty' (Psalm 91:1)?" GotQuestions, accessed March 24, 2026, www.gotquestions.org/shadow-of-the-Almighty.html.

In other words, the psalm isn't a guarantee that we will avoid trials, but a promise that God is present and will sustain us through them. And yet, for those who have walked with God over time, we often witness His literal protection and provision in the midst of danger.

The timing and reasons behind whether God delivers us out of a hardship or carries us through it remain a mystery. But through the lens of the New Testament, we can be confident that the greatest rescue—promised at the end of Psalm 91—is secure: salvation for those who look to Him (verse 16). **In Christ, refuge, protection, and ultimate deliverance are not just hopes—they are guaranteed realities for those who trust in Him.**

What Does the Scripture Mean?

1. What does it mean to practically dwell or abide in God?

2. How is a "fowler" (verse 3) different from the bird metaphors for God in verse 4?

3. What does Ephesians 6:16 tell us about "arrows" and how does this connect to Psalm 91:5? If "arrows" hold a spiritual or metaphorical meaning, what do these look like in everyday life?

4. How does Hebrews 1:14 give greater insight into Psalm 91:11?

5. How does God "flip the script" in verse 14 by shifting from general protection to personal promises for those who love Him? What does this teach us about His relationship with His people?

Connect to the Heart of Jesus

Would it surprise you to know that not only did Jesus quote the psalms in the Gospels but so did Satan? In a chilling scene in the wilderness, Satan tempts Jesus for forty days. At one point, he leads Him to the highest point in Jerusalem and says:

"If you are the Son of God . . .
throw yourself down from here."

(LUKE 4:9)

But Satan doesn't stop there. He even quotes Scripture to try to make his point convincing:

"For it is written: 'He will command his angels concerning you
to guard you carefully; they will lift you up in their hands,
so that you will notstrike your foot against a stone.'"

(VERSES 10–11)

On the surface, it might seem like a good argument. After all, Jesus is the Son of God—He could demonstrate His power, even defeat Satan instantly. But the scene is chilling because it shows how well **Satan knows Scripture and how skillfully he twists it to deceive**.

Jesus sees through the deception and responds with Scripture in proper context, quoting Deuteronomy 6:16:

"It is said, 'Do not put the Lord your God to the test.'"

(LUKE 4:12)

Here we see a profound principle: Jesus loves the psalms, but He also shows us that He doesn't love them being twisted. It is not a tool to test God or justify temptation—even when spoken with the veneer of truth.

But we won't leave off there, with Psalm 91 twisted by Satan, but rather with Jesus who beautifully echoed Psalm 91 in a moving scene in Matthew 23. In

His last public teaching before He is crucified, Jesus rebukes the religious leaders for their spiritual blindness and hypocrisy before turning to His people and saying,

> *"Jerusalem, Jerusalem, you who kill the prophets and stone those sent to you, how often I have longed to gather your children together, as a hen gathers her chicks under her wings, and you were not willing."*
>
> (MATTHEW 23:37–38)

These are words of both rebuke and deep compassion—an expression of the very heart of Psalm 91. The image of a protective bird sheltering her young under her wings comes to life in the person of Jesus. **He longs to gather His people close, to cover them with His mercy, even in the face of rejection.**

What a gracious and patient Savior—one who not only fulfills the promises of Psalm 91 but embodies them. Under His wings, we find the refuge and love that no enemy can twist, and no circumstance can take away.

Apply & Take Action

1. Am I deeply dwelling and resting in God? If not, what might be getting in the way?

2. What does it look like for God's faithfulness to be my shield in my current circumstances (verse 4)?

3. Would the people in my life—at work, at church, in my neighborhood—see that I am someone that "loves" and "acknowledges" God's name (verse 14)?

4. What are some other truths from this psalm that God wants me to take and apply to my life this week?

Pray and ask God to help you apply His truth to your life.

BIBLE BITES for PSALM 91

1. Many Bible scholars think Moses wrote Psalm 91, which would make it **one of the oldest psalms in the Bible**.

2. Psalm 91 has been known as the "Soldier's Psalm" for many years and has been carried by a variety of soldiers.[52]

3. Psalm 91 is prayed by Jewish people as the "Bedtime Shema"—prayers before bed.[53]

52 "Psalm 91: The Soldier's Psalm," Museum of the Bible, May 3, 2021, www.museumofthebible.org/book-minute/psalm-91.

53 Yehuda Shurpin, "What You Need to Know About Going to Bed Like a Jew," Chabad, accessed November 10, 2025, www.chabad.org/library/article_cdo/aid/6955330.

STUDY 27

Unshakeable Roots

Psalm 92

KEY VERSE

It is good to praise the Lord.

(VERSE 1)

Pause . . . pray . . . and ask God for help in today's study.

Who else loves palm trees? There are plenty of reasons to appreciate Psalm 92, but one of my favorites is its use of the palm tree as a metaphor. I already loved palm trees, but after sitting with this psalm, I appreciate them even more. Now, every time I see one, I'm reminded of what the psalmist wanted to show us—a picture of a life that is rooted, flourishing, and thriving. It is no wonder this psalm is the only psalm entitled "For the Sabbath Day," a day that was created by the Lord for the rest and thriving of His people.

Psalm 92 is filled with reminders of what strengthens our souls and helps us grow with resilience and joy. **It's a psalm about spiritual vitality, and the palm tree becomes a living symbol of the kind of life God invites us to experience.**

So whether you're a palm-tree person, a pine-tree person, or someone who just tries to keep your houseplants alive, the message is the same: God wants our lives to flourish. And thankfully, unlike me with my houseplants, He's really good at making that happen.

Look Deeper

Open your Bible and **read Psalm 92** at least once.

1. What attributes and actions of God through the psalm support the first statement, "It is good to praise the LORD"? What things does the psalm point to about God that make it good to praise Him?

2. What does the psalmist indicate brings him joy and helps him thrive?

The psalmist—an unnamed author—opens Psalm 92 with a simple but powerful reminder: "It is good to praise the LORD." He describes a life that begins the day proclaiming God's love and ends by remembering His faithfulness. Our first instinct might be to assume it's "good" because God is worthy of our praise (and He absolutely is). But the psalmist gives another reason in verses 4–5: He's filled with gladness because of what God has done. He praises because God's works bring him joy.

In other words, **praising God isn't only good for Him, it's deeply good for us.** It does something in our souls. And interestingly, modern research is finally catching up with what Scripture has been saying for thousands of years. Studies on gratitude—which Christians sometimes refer to as praise and thanksgiving—show that practicing thankfulness actually boosts our emotional health. It increases serotonin and dopamine, those mood-lifting, stabilizing hormones our brain loves.[54]

So, when the psalmist begins with "It is good to praise the LORD," he isn't just giving us a checkbox—he's inviting us into something that heals, strengthens, and nourishes us from the inside out. And the rest of the psalm flows from this foundation, as the psalmist continues to reflect on the goodness of God—such as His works and thoughts (verse 5), His exaltation (verse 8), and His justice (verses 9–11).

And the psalmist continues to tell us about true flourishing:

> *The righteous will flourish like a palm tree, they will grow like a cedar of Lebanon; planted in the house of the LORD, they will flourish in the courts of our God.*
>
> (VERSE 12–13)

---

54 American Brain Foundation, "Does Gratitude Rewire Your Brain?" accessed March 24, 2026, https://www.americanbrainfoundation.org/does-gratitude-rewire-your-brain/.

According to the psalmist, those who root their lives in God and walk in His ways flourish like a palm tree. If you've ever seen footage of a hurricane, you may have noticed that while almost everything else is flattened, the palm trees are still standing. Their secret is in their roots—dense, widespread, and designed to anchor them when the world around them is shaking. A palm tree bends, sways, and takes a beating, but it doesn't break. And even more fascinating, its trunk is firm on the outside but soft and flexible on the inside, making it incredibly adaptable when the winds hit hard.

The psalmist adds another layer to this picture: The righteous also "grow like a cedar of Lebanon" (verse 12)—trees known in biblical times for their enormous height, their strength, and their durability.[55]

And then comes the encouragement many of us need to hear: The righteous don't just flourish when they're young and energetic. They are people who, even in old age, "bear fruit" and "stay fresh and green" (verse 14). Their lives continue to matter, continue to give, and continue to point others to God's faithfulness. I don't know about you, but I don't want to grow in crankiness and purposelessness as I age. And the Bible tells us we don't have to.

We'll dive deeper into these metaphors as we continue our study, but for now, the psalmist's message is simple and powerful: A flourishing life isn't about having perfect circumstances—it's about being rooted in the right place.

What Does the Scripture Mean?

1. We briefly discussed why it is "good" to praise the Lord. What else does this mean? What are some practical ways it is good to praise the Lord?

55 "Psalm 92," Bible Hub, accessed December 3, 2025, https://biblehub.com/commentaries/benson/psalms/92.htm.

2. What does it mean when it says "evildoers flourish" (verse 7)? What is a biblical example as well as an example in today's world?

3. How and why does the psalmist contrast fools and senseless people with God (verses 6–8)?

4. What might it mean for the righteous to have a strong structure and yet still be flexible within?

Connect to the Heart of Jesus

Psalm 92 was written for and points us back to the meaning of the Sabbath, which was a special sign God established with Israel:

> *"'The Israelites are to observe the Sabbath, celebrating it for the generations to come as a lasting covenant. It will be a sign between me and the Israelites forever, for in six days the LORD made the heavens and the earth, and on the seventh day he rested and was refreshed.'"*
>
> (EXODUS 31:16–17)

The Sabbath was given so that God's people would stop their labor and experience true rest. Today, Christians hold a variety of views on how literally the Sabbath should be observed, but Scripture consistently points to the deeper significance behind it: **The Sabbath was always meant to foreshadow the coming of Jesus,** the One who would bring permanent, soul-level rest to His people.

The endless cycle of sacrifices, the work of imperfect priests, and Israel's constant striving to remain acceptable before God has been replaced by something far better—the perfect and eternal High Priest, Jesus Christ. Through His once-for-all sacrifice and His finished work on the cross, He accomplished what the Sabbath pointed toward:

But when this priest had offered for
all time one sacrifice for sins,
he sat down at the right hand of God.

(HEBREWS 10:12)

In Christ, the true rest promised in the Sabbath has finally arrived. Instead of relying on temporary sacrifices to make us right with God, **Jesus became our righteousness—once and for all**—so that we could continually flourish like the palm tree and grow strong like the cedar through His Spirit.

Psalm 92 may have been sung once a week on the Sabbath, but because of Jesus its message is meant to be sung in the rhythm of our everyday lives. This isn't just a weekly song anymore—it's a way of being. A song written on our hearts. A melody that shapes how we work, rest, worship, love, and live.

Because Jesus has brought us true rest, our joy should rise even higher than the psalmist's because we can say with confidence and gratitude:

For you make me glad by your deeds, Lord;
I sing for joy at what your hands have done.

(PSALM 92:4)

Our rest is secure. Our flourishing is possible. Our joy is rooted in Him. And that is a song worth singing with our whole lives.

Apply & Take Action

1. How can I praise the Lord right now, even in the midst of difficulties I might be facing? What can I thank Him for right now?

2. What is something He has done in the past for me that can give me joy today (verse 4)?

3. What aspects of the metaphors of the palm and cedar trees do I want to see more in my life?

4. Am I bearing more fruit as I age? Am I becoming fresher and greener—maybe not physically but spiritually—as I age (verse 14)?

Pray and ask God to help you apply His truth to your life.

BIBLE BITES for PSALM 92

1. Psalm 92 is sung in the temple every Sabbath morning.[56]

2. At the time when this psalm was written, only the priests were allowed in the "courts of our God" (verse 13). This was a beautiful foreshadowing of the New Testament when God would be constantly dwelling with every believer.

3. A "horn," mentioned in verse 10, was a symbol of strength and might in the Bible.

56 Mishnah Tamid, https://www.sefaria.org/Mishnah_Tamid.7.1?lang=bi.

STUDY 28

Mighty Waters, Mighty God

Psalm 93

KEY VERSE

Mightier than the thunder of the great waters,
mightier than the breakers of the sea—the LORD on high is mighty.

(VERSE 4)

Pause . . . pray . . . and ask God for help in today's study.

Our psalm today may be short, but it's (literally) mighty. Last time, we explored the palm tree metaphor, and today we're riding the waves with metaphors of the sea. Now, I'd like to think this is God's subtle way of telling us that a tropical vacation is calling our names—but the truth is even better. These images of waves and the sea point us to something far deeper and more lasting than a short getaway: They reveal the power, majesty, and steadfastness of God in the midst of life's storms.

Look Deeper

Open your Bible and read Psalm 93 at least once.

1. What truths about God does the author use to understand this psalm?

2. How do the truths about God in this psalm shed light on the nature of humanity?

No matter our culture, generation, or place in history, there is one reality that unites us all: Governments and their leaders are ever-changing, and none of them can truly be trusted. Perhaps you, like me, have put your hope and trust in a governing leader only to experience disappointment a short time later. And it's within that shared uncertainty and disappointment that Psalm 93 speaks so boldly:

The LORD reigns, he is robed in majesty;
the LORD is robed in majesty and armed with strength;
indeed, the world is established, firm and secure.
Your throne was established long ago;
you are from all eternity.

(VERSES 1–2)

While we may not know the exact time Psalm 93 was written, we do know that **the world of the Psalms was marked by unstable governments and corrupt leaders**—even among God's own people. It's a reality that still feels so familiar today. Yet Psalm 93 reminds us that even a few simple words of Scripture can carry immense weight and hope: The Lord reigns. He reigned in the midst of chaos in the Old Testament, and He reigns today, in the midst of the uncertainty and turmoil of our own world. And yet God has established the world—"firm and secure" (verse 1)—and it can only be moved by Him.

As echoed later in Isaiah 44:6, "I am the first and I am the last; apart from me there is no God," the author declares the everlasting and eternal nature of God: "Your throne was established long ago; you are from all eternity" (Psalm 93:2). **World and government leaders rise and fall, but God's throne is established forever.**

And even if the ocean doesn't captivate you as it does me, the next stanza offers a beautiful poetic metaphor: The pounding waves, which seem to rise up in defiance, lift their voices as if challenging God (verse 3), but God—"the LORD on high" (verse 4)—reigns above all. The most powerful wave ever recorded by humans occurred on July 9, 1958, in Lituya Bay, in southeast Alaska, when an earthquake struck the Alaskan panhandle along the Fairweather fault line. The 7.8-magnitude earthquake shook loose a massive chunk of rock above Lituya Bay, causing nearly forty million cubic yards of the mountainside to crash into the water.[57]

---

57 Zach Taras, "The Largest Tsunami Ever Recorded Only Claimed 2 Lives," How Stuff Works, August 22, 2024, https://science.howstuffworks.com/nature/natural-disasters/largest-tsunami-ever-recorded.htm.

And God is still mightier than the waves of the sea, the strongest tsunami to ever be recorded.

Seemingly abruptly, the psalmist transitions from the waves of the sea to the trustworthiness of God's decrees—His Word. But this is when it all comes together. We can know about Him through His creation—that He is powerful and mighty, but it's His Word that tells us the intimate details of His heart and who He is. His Word speaks the clarity of what creation is telling us.

What Does the Scripture Mean?

1. What does it mean when it says God "has put on strength as his belt" (verse 1 ESV)?

2. How do we reconcile the chaos of the world with the truths in Psalm 93—that the Lord reigns?

3. Why might the psalmist transition from talking about God's power over the waves to how trustworthy His decrees are?

Connect to the Heart of Jesus

We already revisited the story of Jesus sleeping during the storm in study 3, but it's worth bringing up again—because now we get to see how that moment becomes a literal picture of God's power over the waves. It's also **the only place in the entire Bible where we see Jesus sleeping**. And honestly, it's almost comical: The disciples are panicking, water is crashing into the boat, chaos is everywhere . . . and there's Jesus asleep, basically wearing what I imagine as a "Do Not Disturb" sign on His forehead.

But, of course they wake Him. (And who can blame them, given the kind of waves we're talking about?) And with just a word, Jesus proves He is truly "mightier than the waves of the sea" (Psalm 93:4 ESV), silencing the wind and the waves with a rebuke (Mark 4:35–41).

Later, Jesus calls Peter out onto similar waters in Matthew 14. Peter had already watched Jesus silence the storm—so shouldn't he have had the faith to believe Jesus could handle it again? And to his credit, Peter does step out of the boat. Maybe he is remembering what Jesus had already done. But then Peter—very much like many of us (hand raised over here, too)—starts doubting again "when he [sees] the wind" (Matthew 14:30), and he begins to sink.

That darn wind. Always stirring fear.

And then comes this incredibly tender moment. Jesus could've spoken another command and lifted Peter up instantly. But instead, the text tells us He reaches out His hand and grabs hold of him. "'You of little faith,' he said, 'why did you doubt?'" (verse 31).

Jesus gives us the living, breathing expression of Psalm 93. He's mightier than the physical waves, but also the waves we face every day: mightier than the circumstantial waves, the emotional waves, and the relational waves.

He doesn't always pull us out of the waves—but He always walks us through them. And not from a distance, but with His hand.

Through creation—and His authority over it—He shows His power. But through His trustworthy words, His decrees, He speaks to our fear. It's there He reminds us we don't have to panic when the waves rise. It's where He says:

"Come to me, all you who are weary and burdened, and I will give you rest."

(MATTHEW 11:28)

Apply & Take Action

1. What circumstantial, emotional, or relational waves am I facing right now? How can the truth about God's mightiness over those things bring me comfort?

2. What truth in God's decrees might speak into my waves right now?

3. Is there any part of me struggling with fear right now? What does it look like to practice taking the hand of Jesus?

4. What specifically does God want me to apply to my life this week from this psalm?

Pray and ask God to help you apply His truth to your life.

BIBLE BITES for PSALM 93

1. Paul David Tripp entitled Psalm 93 "The Reign of the King" and suggested it be read every morning.[58]

2. Psalm 93 is said to be part of the "Enthronement Psalms," Psalms 93–100, which emphasize God's reign.[59]

3. Notice how Psalm 93 can echo Genesis 1—when God brought order to the waters.

58 Paul Tripp, "Psalm 93: The Reign of the King," Paul Tripp Ministries, February 12, 2024, www.paultripp.com/psalms/posts/psalm-93-the-reign-of-the-king.

59 "Enthronement Psalms," Psalms.org, accessed March 24, 2026, https://psalms.org/psalms/category/enthronement.

STUDY 29

The Key to Rest: A Softened Heart

Psalm 95

KEY VERSE

Today, if you hear his voice, do not harden your hearts.

(VERSES 7–8 ESV)

Pause . . . pray . . . and ask God for help in today's study.

Have you ever noticed that the best Bible commentary out there . . . is actually the Bible itself? **One of the richest ways to understand Scripture is when Scripture explains or builds on itself.** Today's psalm gives us such a gift. Hebrews 3–4 reads almost like an ancient Bible commentary on Psalm 95.

James Montgomery Boice commented on the Hebrews passage: "This is probably the most thorough citing of an Old Testament passage in the New Testament."[60] And honestly, it feels like we get to sit shoulder-to-shoulder with the author of Hebrews, walking through Psalm 95 together. What a joy to study not just about God, but with the help of God's own Word.

Look Deeper

Open your Bible and **read Psalm 95** at least once.

1. What truths about God stand out to you from this psalm?

2. What stands out to you about the heart of man in this passage?

Some psalms dive straight into deep lament, but others—like Psalm 95—waste no time launching into full-on, joy-filled praise. Right from the start, **the psalmist calls God's people to worship together,** using the phrase "let us" three different times in just the first two verses. It's a reminder that worshiping God

60 James Montgomery Boice, quoted in David Guzik, *Enduring Word Commentary*, "Psalm 95," accessed December 9, 2025, https://enduringword.com/bible-commentary/psalm-95/.

with others isn't just a feel-good moment with the music swelling and voices harmonizing. It's actually a biblical invitation—and a biblical command.

Then the psalmist gives us the why behind the worship. In short: **God is greater than everything else, and one of the clearest ways He shows this is through His creation**—specifically, the seas. This is the second psalm in a row that highlights God's power over the waters (remember Psalm 93?), and there's a reason for that. The sea was necessary for travel and trade, but in the ancient world it was also terrifying.

As the Bible Odyssey scholars note, ancient records show over a thousand known shipwreck sites across the Mediterranean, and some estimate that nearly one-fifth of sea journeys faced serious danger.[61] For the Israelites—who rarely traveled by sea—the ocean wasn't romantic or adventurous (or fun like my surf days); it was one of the most fear-inducing forces in their world, and it would bring great comfort to know God ruled the seas.

But the psalmist doesn't stop there. Not only does God reign over the seas; He also created us. He's "our Maker" (verse 6). And unlike the seas, we're not just natural elements under His command—we're His people, "the flock under his care" (verse 7). His creative powers reached us in a personal, intimate way. And with that personal connection the psalmist gives a warning:

"Do not harden your hearts as you did at Meribah,
as you did that day at Massah in the wilderness."

(VERSE 8)

The psalmist is saying, essentially: If God rules the seas . . . if He created you . . . if He shepherds you . . . then why would you resist His voice? Why repeat the mistakes of your ancestors—those who complained at Meribah (Numbers

61 Troy M. Troftgruben, "Sea Travel and Shipwrecks in the Ancient World," Bible Odyssey, accessed December 9, 2025, www.bibleodyssey.org/articles/sea-travel-and-shipwrecks-in-the-ancient-world.

20:1–3) and refused to trust God when it was time to enter the promised land (Numbers 13–14)?

Then comes the sobering final line:

"'They shall never enter my rest.'"

(VERSE 11)

It feels abrupt, even harsh, especially after such an endearing beginning. But it makes sense: **If God is that powerful and that caring, then obeying Him isn't a burden, it's the natural response of people who know their Shepherd.** Our obedience (imperfect as it is) becomes the evidence that we're living under His care.

What Does the Scripture Mean?

1. What does verse 4 mean, "In his hand are the depths of the earth"?

2. How does this psalm present a picture of the relationship between joy and obedience?

3. How does the psalm move from praise (verses 1–7) to warning (verses 8–11)? What is the meaning of this progression?

Connect to the Heart of Jesus

As mentioned in the introduction, Hebrews 3–4 is our very own commentary on Psalm 95, and it's worth reading (if you have time) or at least keeping open alongside this section. And one of the things that the author of Hebrews does is tell us the author of Psalm 95, listing not one but two authors. Hebrews 3:7 tells us, "So, as the Holy Spirit says . . . " and in 4:7 the author tells us God "spoke through David" again in reference to the psalm. What a beautiful reminder that Scripture was penned by men who were "carried along by the Holy Spirit" (2 Peter 1:21).

And did you notice the author of Hebrews speaks in the present in reference to the Holy Spirit speaking? I love that this reminds us **Psalm 95 isn't just about the past, it's for our today**. It speaks directly into our lives right now: "Today, if you hear his voice, do not harden your hearts" (verses 7–8 ESV).

Hebrews takes the warning from Psalm 95 and deepens it. The Israelites hardened their hearts toward Moses, but we are faced with the opportunity to make an even greater mistake—we can harden our hearts toward Jesus Himself. The author describes this as "a sinful, unbelieving heart that turns away from the living God" (Hebrews 3:12). As I sat with that, I was reminded (and honestly humbled) that this doesn't always look like obvious rebellion. For the

Israelites, it showed up in complaining and not trusting God's provision. For us, it can be more subtle like questioning His goodness, wondering if He'll really come through, or placing our hope in other things before Him.

But this passage in Hebrews doesn't just continue with the warning we found in Psalm 95; it gives us a way forward. We are told to "encourage one another daily" (Hebrews 3:13), reminding us that keeping our hearts soft isn't something we're meant to do alone. We need people who will speak truth into our lives and help us stay soft to God's voice. Along with that, we are called to "hold our original conviction firmly to the very end" (verse 14), continually coming back to what we know is true about Jesus and choosing not to let go of Him.

As the author moves into chapter 4, he makes it even clearer what keeps us from entering God's rest: unbelief. It's not mainly a lack of effort or discipline, but a struggle to trust Him. And this is where everything comes together. The "rest" in Psalm 95:11 is not just a place or a future promise, it's found in a person, Jesus. True rest means letting go of striving to earn God's approval and no longer carrying the pressure to prove ourselves. It's learning to trust in the finished work of Christ and rely on what He has already done rather than what we can do. And the author makes it clear how we enter that rest: "Now we who have believed enter that rest" (Hebrews 4:3).

If I'm honest, I still feel that tension between belief and unbelief in my own heart at times. Maybe you do, too. And when that tension shows up, I find myself coming back to a simple, honest prayer from the Gospels: "I do believe; help me overcome my unbelief!" (Mark 9:24).

Apply & Take Action

1. Is there any unbelief in my heart toward God or His promises? How can this psalm speak into my unbelief today?

2. How can I encourage someone today to live out the exhortation to "encourage one another daily" (Hebrews 3:13)?

3. Is there any part of God's Word that I have read or heard, but am not obeying?

Pray and ask God to help you apply His truth to your life.

BIBLE BITES for PSALM 95

1. ***Meribah***—the place referenced in Psalm 95 where the Israelites complained—means "quarrel, strife, or dispute" in Hebrew.

2. ***Massah***—the place referenced in Psalm 95 where the Israelites tested the Lord in the wilderness—means "testing" in Hebrew.

3. Psalm 95 is part of the "Kabbalat Shabbat"—psalms quoted at the beginning of Jewish services.[62]

62 Mendel Adelman, "What Is Kabbalat Shabbat?" Chabad, accessed December 9, 2025, www.chabad.org/library/article_cdo/aid/6430392.

STUDY 30

Joy to Our Weary World and Hearts

Psalm 98

KEY VERSE

Shout for joy to the LORD, all the earth.

(VERSE 4)

Pause . . . pray . . . and ask God for help in today's study.

You're probably familiar with the beloved Christmas song "Joy to the World," one of the most widely sung carols across the world. But did you know that every time you've belted it out (for me, that means loud and off-key), you've actually been singing words inspired by Psalm 98?

"Joy to the World" holds the title of the most published Christmas carol in North America and was written in 1719 by English minister and hymnist Isaac Watts.[63] Interestingly, Watts didn't originally write it as a Christmas song at all—it was his poetic reflection on Psalm 98 and the triumphant coming of the Lord. Which means, technically, it's a hymn that can be sung year-round—a song, not just for December, but for every season that calls for joy (so . . . all of them). And I think we will see why as we dive into these words.

Look Deeper

Open your Bible and **read Psalm 98** at least once.

1. What are some truths about God the author is communicating through this psalm?

2. What stands out to you about mankind in this psalm?

63 Sian Moore, "What are the lyrics to 'Joy to the World', who composed the carol and what does it mean?" ClassicFM, November 23, 2021, https://www.classicfm.com/discover-music/occasions/christmas/joy-to-the-world-hymn-carol-lyrics-composer/.

We've walked through a lot of lament in our journey through the psalms—grief, questions, and honest wrestling with God. But now, in Psalm 98, the tone shifts completely. Our gaze and affections are lifted toward unhindered praise and joy. Every line of this psalm bursts with celebration. It opens with the words "Sing to the LORD a new song," as if to say, there isn't a song in existence big enough to hold this kind of joy. We don't always know what to do with exuberant emotion, especially in faith spaces that often value calm and composure. Maybe you feel that way yourself in most public spaces, but have you ever had a moment in your walk with God when you have felt as though the joy you were experiencing about Him or about what He has done is indescribable, almost as though you could burst? This psalm speaks even to the heart of the one that might describe himself as unemotional, encouraging us to "burst into jubilant song" (verse 4).

The psalmist doesn't hold back—he overflows with awe and excitement at what God has done. His praise is grounded, not in hype or mood, but in the reality that God's "right hand and his holy arm have worked salvation for him" (verse 1). In other words, **God has acted—and that action calls for a response that can't stay quiet.** As you read through these words, you hopefully have seen why Isaac Watts chose this psalm to write "Joy to the World," and also why it has shifted to be such a popular Christmas song, since Psalm 98 centers upon God's salvation.

The author centers upon the universal invitation of salvation "to the nations" (verse 2)—which probably would have blown some of the Israelites' minds as they had been a chosen race, a chosen people by God. But **God was continuing to reveal His love and plan for the world**—to call people to Himself from every tribe, tongue, and nation. No wonder the psalmist rejoiced.

Joy had come to the world.

What Does the Scripture Mean?

1. How does the psalm connect God's actions in Israel with the hope of all nations?

2. What does it mean that "the LORD has made his salvation known and revealed his righteousness to the nations" (verse 2)? How did He do that at the time this psalm was written, and how does He do that today?

3. What does it mean that the sea, rivers, and mountains are personified as rejoicing (verse 7–8), and what does this say about the relationship between creation and God?

4. What might it mean that "He will judge the world in righteousness and the peoples with equity" (verse 9)?

Connect to the Heart of Jesus

Although Psalm 98 looks ahead prophetically to the coming of Jesus, that promise wouldn't be fulfilled for roughly five hundred to one thousand years—depending on whether the psalm was written during David's reign or after the Babylonian exile. And in that long stretch of time came what's often called the four hundred years of silence—no new psalms, no fresh words from the prophets, no obvious sign of God speaking. You can imagine the questions that must have filled people's hearts during that time: Where is the Messiah we've been waiting for? Has God forgotten His promises? Generations were born and died clinging to hope, yet they never saw it fulfilled.

But then, at just the right time, everything changed. Luke writes that because of God's tender mercy, "the rising sun [that] will come to us from heaven" began to rise out of that long night of silence (Luke 1:78). And the first voice to break that silence in song wasn't a prophet or a famous king—it was a poor, young woman named Mary, who of course we now know was Jesus' mom. Her song later titled the Magnificat in Luke 1:46–55 became the first recorded song of praise after centuries of waiting—a joyful echo of Psalm 98.[64]

---

64 Jason Gaboury, "The Power of Praying the Magnificat Daily," March 8, 2017, https://intervarsity.org/blog/2017/power-praying-magnificat-daily.

Just as Psalm 98 celebrates God's salvation, faithfulness, and righteous judgment made visible to all nations (Psalm 98:2–3, 9), Mary's song rejoices in those same truths. Where the psalm calls for a "new song" of praise for God's saving power (verse 1), **Mary becomes the living answer to that call—singing of God's mercy and His faithfulness to Israel** (Luke 1:46–55). Both proclaim a God who lifts up the humble and brings justice to the world (Psalm 98:9; Luke 1:51–52), revealing His salvation for all people (Psalm 98:3; Luke 2:30–32).

Does this just blow your mind as it did mine? In many ways, Mary's song is the new song the psalmist called for—the moment when centuries of longing finally turned into praise for . . .

Joy to the world, Jesus has come!

Apply & Take Action

1. Do I feel joyful today over my salvation through Jesus? In what ways do I need God to restore my joy over His salvation (Psalm 51:12)?

2. In what ways is God calling me to be a part of bringing and furthering salvation to the nations?

3. Who is someone specifically in my life that needs me to share the message of salvation with them? How will I share it with them?

Pray and ask God to help you apply His truth to your life.

BIBLE BITES for PSALM 98

1. Psalm 98 is one of the few psalms that doesn't include a lament or petition.

2. Psalm 98 is part of a group of **royal psalms** that celebrate God as King over all the earth.

3. Not only did Isaac Watts not intend for "Joy to the World" to be a Christmas song, but he didn't intend it to be a song at all and initially wrote it as a poem.[65]

65 Greg Forster, "A Brief History of 'Joy to the World,'" Crossway, accessed March 24, 2026, www.crossway.org/articles/a-brief-history-of-joy-to-the-world.

STUDY 31

Our Great Shepherd

Psalm 100

KEY VERSE

We are his people, the sheep of his pasture.

(VERSE 3)

Pause . . . pray . . . and ask God for help in today's study.

Just when you thought the praise music from Psalm 98 was ending, Psalm 100 cranks it back up. Psalm 100 is one of the shortest psalms but has one of the most powerful and familiar metaphors for God in the Bible—He is our shepherd. In the Old Testament, there are approximately eight to ten direct references to God being our shepherd (varies depending on literal or metaphorical mention), and there are around eight direct references to Jesus as our shepherd in the New Testament. The metaphor is powerful because sheep are dependent. And **it's in this dependency on the Shepherd that we see the heart of God.**

Look Deeper

Open your Bible and read Psalm 100 at least once.

1. Reflect on all that you know about shepherds. What do you learn about God through this metaphor in Psalm 100?

2. Reflect on all you know about sheep. What does this teach you about people, and specifically those who follow God?

You may have noticed while reading Psalm 100 that it opens with a familiar call from Psalm 98:4: "Shout for joy to the LORD, all the earth" (verse 1). We're not told who wrote Psalm 100, but it's easy to imagine it coming from the same heart behind Psalm 98—or at least from someone who wanted to continue the praise party. Like the psalmist of Psalm 98, **this writer wants our hearts to be stirred** "with gladness" as we worship (verse 2). And right in the middle of the joy party comes a powerful reminder: "Know that the LORD is God" (verse 3).

Charles Spurgeon wrote of this verse,

> We ought to know whom we worship and why . . . it is very questionable whether a man can know himself until he knows his God.[66]

Doesn't that hit hard? Because it's true—our worship isn't just about singing; it's about remembering who God is and, in turn, who we are.

The psalmist continues, "It is he who made us, and we are his" (verse 3). That short phrase—"we are his"—might be one of the most beautiful truths in all of Scripture. We belong to Him. The same God who knit us together in our mother's womb (Psalm 139:13–14) designed us with care, purpose, and love. And in a world that's constantly telling us to find or reinvent ourselves, or find our individuality first in our careers, our gender, our sexual identity, our influence, and so much more—Psalm 100 brings us back to something far more stable, truthful, and freeing: **Our identity isn't something we earn, perform, or invent—it's something we receive. We are His.**

And here in verse 3 the psalmist uses two distinct names for God: LORD and God. "LORD," in all capital letters, translates to the sacred name Yahweh—the personal, covenant name of God, revealing His intimate relationship with His people. "God," on the other hand, comes from the Hebrew word *Elohim*—a title that emphasizes His power, majesty, and sovereignty over all creation.

By using both names together, the psalmist reminds us that **the One we worship is not a distant or generic deity, but Yahweh Elohim**—the all-powerful Creator who also knows us personally, lovingly, and by name.

---

66 Charles Spurgeon, "Psalm 100," Blue Letter Bible, accessed November 12, 2025, https://www.blueletterbible.org/Comm/spurgeon_charles/tod/ps100.cfm.

While our previous study in Psalm 98 reaches its climax in a global celebration—joy to the world that God's salvation is coming to every tribe, tongue, and nation—Psalm 100 brings that joy close to home. It culminates in the deeply personal and intimate truth that we belong to God—not only as individuals, but together as His people.

What Does the Scripture Mean?

1. What does it mean to **worship or serve the Lord with gladness even when challenges come**—whether circumstantially or relationally—in the things we do?

2. What is the significance of the phrase to "Know that the LORD is God" (verse 3), even while being a believer? What does this look like in practice?

3. Why might the exhortation to "enter his gates with thanksgiving" (verse 4) follow the promise that we are His? What might "his gates" be compared to in our modern world?

4. What does it mean that God's love endures forever? Knowing the historical context of the psalms, why might this have been a significant truth to communicate?

Connect to the Heart of Jesus

In one of the clearest fulfillments of Psalm 100:3, Jesus—both as our shepherd and as God Himself—declares,

"I am the good shepherd; I know my sheep and my sheep know me."

(JOHN 10:14)

As mentioned earlier, sheep are perceptive. Yet they remain completely dependent on their shepherd. That combination of intelligence and dependence makes them a profoundly beautiful metaphor for us. And while we reflect on what it means for God to be our shepherd and for us to be His sheep, what we may overlook is that **sheep aren't only dependent on their shepherd—they're also deeply dependent on one another.**

Studies show that when separated from their flock, sheep experience emotional distress—even depression.[67] They were designed for connection. And so were we.

---

67 Kalyan De et al., "Effect of Short-Term Seclusion of Sheep on Their Welfare Indicators," *Journal of Veterinary Behavior* 25 (2018), 42–47, https://doi.org/10.1016/j.jveb.2018.05.007.

In the New Testament, the phrase "one another" appears roughly a hundred times, translated from the Greek word *allelon*.[68] Many of these commands come directly from Jesus Himself—urging us to love one another, forgive one another, honor one another, and serve one another. In other words, **one of the ways our Great Shepherd cares for us is by leading us into interdependence.** Jesus doesn't just command us to care for one another—He created us to need one another. Our souls were designed to thrive in community.

Psalm 100 reminds us that it isn't only "I am His" but also "We are his" (verse 3)—a collective flock under the gentle, faithful care of our Shepherd.

So, it's no surprise that as our world drifts further into isolation and division, our mental health suffers deeply.[69] We were never meant to walk alone. We were made to be shepherded by the Shepherd, together.

Apply & Take Action

1. Has it been easy or hard lately to worship or serve the Lord with gladness? **How might I need more gladness restored** in what I am called to?

68 Strong's Greek 240, ἀλλήλων (*allelōn*): one another, each other.

69 "APA Poll Reveals a Nation Suffering from Stress of Societal Division, Loneliness," American Psychological Association, November 6, 2025, www.apa.org/news/press/releases/2025/11/nation-suffering-division-loneliness.

2. How might verse 3 encourage me in my doubts? Who else in my life needs to be encouraged to *know* that He is God?

3. What image of God as our shepherd hits me most? In what ways am I tempted to operate in self-sufficiency rather than in dependence upon my Father?

4. Is my life marked by thanksgiving, or am I struggling with discontentment?

Pray and ask God to help you apply His truth to your life.

BIBLE BITES for PSALM 100

1. Psalm 100 is the only psalm titled as a psalm for giving thanks or praise.

2. The poetry in Psalm 100 is incredibly symmetrical—giving repeated calls to praise and reasons for our praise.

3. Psalm 100 has been the inspiration for countless hymns and songs over the years.

STUDY 32

When God First Introduced Himself

Psalm 103

KEY VERSE

He made known his ways to Moses, his deeds to the people of Israel.

(VERSE 7)

Pause . . . pray . . . and ask God for help in today's study.

This is the final psalm we will study in Book IV of Psalms, and it is absolutely drenched in the love of God. I'll never forget one Sunday when one of my worship leaders stood up and read a passage, pointing out that **these were the very words God first used to introduce Himself**.

Wait—what? God introducing Himself? I remember thinking. Those were the words I longed to hear. Have you ever wondered what words God would use to introduce Himself?

David gives us a glimpse midway through this psalm. Those words form the very foundation of the entire psalm.

Look Deeper

Open your Bible and read Psalm 103 at least once.

1. Since it was built up in the introduction, what words did God use when He "made known his ways to Moses" (verse 7), and what does this tell you about God (see Exodus 34:6–7)? How are these characteristics of God celebrated in this psalm?

2. What does the metaphor in verses 15–16 reveal about mankind?

Psalm 103 opens with effusive praise as David calls his soul to bless the Lord and remember His goodness. The psalmist recounts God's compassion, forgiveness, and steadfast love with such warmth that it can be easy to imagine him as someone who lived in a constant state of spiritual enthusiasm. But tucked within those opening lines is a revealing phrase: "Forget not all his benefits" (verse 2).

This small command reminds us of a deeper truth that continues to be revealed in our psalms studies—**David praised God not because he never struggled, but because he knew how easily his heart could drift into forgetfulness**. His worship was not the automatic overflow of a perfectly disciplined soul; it was the intentional choice of someone aware of his own tendency to overlook God's mercy.

In other words, even the man after God's own heart had to remind himself to remember. And as David keeps going, he doesn't just list God's "benefits"—he reaches all the way back to the moment God first revealed Himself in Exodus. He intentionally brings to mind God's compassion, forgiveness, and grace, and of course he has to add, "so great is his love" (verse 11), because that's who God has always been.

By the time he ends the psalm, David zooms out to show the massive scope of who should praise God: the angels, all of creation, everyone who follows Him—"everywhere in his dominion" (verse 22). And then he pulls it right back in, making it personal: "Praise the LORD, my soul" (verse 22). David reminds us that worship starts out there, but it also starts right here, inside our own hearts.

What Does the Scripture Mean?

1. How does forgetfulness threaten our relationship with God, according to the psalm?

2. What is the significance of the imagery of human life being like "dust" or a "flower of the field" (verses 14–16)?

3. What does it mean that God's love is "from everlasting to everlasting . . . with those who keep his covenant" (verses 17–18)?

4. How does obedience relate to experiencing the blessings David describes (see verses 17–18)?

5. How does David describe God's justice for "all the oppressed" (verse 6), and what does that reveal about God's priorities?

Connect to the Heart of Jesus

Psalm 103 didn't just echo in David's lifetime—it echoed and sang for generations. It even shaped the words of Mary, the mother of Jesus, when she sang her own song of praise, the Magnificat:

"His mercy extends to those who fear him,
from generation to generation."

(LUKE 1:50)

Mary had just heard from the angel Gabriel that she would bear a son—the Son of the Most High—the promised King who would sit on David's throne and whose kingdom would never end (Luke 1:32–33).

Imagine what must have gone through Mary's mind as she processed this news through the lens of Psalm 103. David—her ancestor many generations removed, as in great-great-grandfather many times over—had sung about the mercy and steadfast love of God, and about the promise of a coming Messiah from his line. Now Mary was watching that promise unfold, not just in her family tree, but within her own body. The words of Psalm 103 weren't just poetic anymore—they were becoming reality. From David's generation to hers and far beyond, God was proving Himself faithful and merciful.

And then, in the only place where Jesus explicitly describes His own heart, He says, "I am gentle and humble in heart" (Matthew 11:29). **Jesus is the living embodiment of the mercy David celebrated and Mary echoed.** He is the exact expression of the God who first revealed Himself as "compassionate and gracious . . . slow to anger, abounding in love and faithfulness" (Exodus 34:6).

How can our souls not join with David's in singing, "Praise the LORD, my soul" (Psalm 103:22)?

Apply & Take Action

1. Of all the "benefits" of God mentioned in this psalm, which is hardest for me to believe? How can I walk in that truth more?

2. What is the first thing that comes to my mind when I think about God? Theologian A. W. Tozer said, "What comes into our minds when we think about God is the most important thing about us."[70] Do I agree? Why or why not?

3. How does my relationship with my earthly father affect how I read verse 13? Are there ways I need my view of a father healed?

70 Randy Alcorn, "The Most Important Thing About Us," Eternal Perspectives Ministries, 2013. https://www.epm.org/resources/2013/May/6/tozer/.

Pray and ask God to help you apply His truth to your life.

BIBLE BITES for PSALM 103

1. Psalm 103 is one of the few psalms with no requests—just all praise.

2. Charles Spurgeon called Psalm 103 a "Bible in itself."[71]

3. Psalm 103 is believed to have been **written in David's later years**—offering praise even after a lifetime of various trials.

71 Charles Spurgeon, "Psalm 103," Spurgeon Archive, accessed November 14, 2025, https://archive.spurgeon.org/treasury/ps103.php.

STUDY 33

Eavesdropping on Eternity

Psalm 110

KEY VERSE

The LORD says to my lord: "Sit at my right hand until I make your enemies a footstool for your feet."

(VERSE 1)

Pause . . . pray . . . and ask God for help in today's study.

We're jumping into our first psalm from Book V, and this one is strikingly unique. Psalm 110 is quoted or referenced around twenty-seven times in the New Testament—more than any other psalm. **Jesus quoted it twice**. And just like we saw with Psalm 95, the author of Hebrews gives us an entire section unpacking it through some commentary (Hebrews 7:11–28). At this point, it should be pretty obvious the writer of Hebrews really loved the psalms.

Psalm 110 is a messianic psalm, which means we get to explore how the apostles, prophets, and Jesus saw it as a powerful picture of who the Messiah truly is. It's one of those places in Scripture where **the Old and New Testaments show their seamless partnership,** giving us a deeper look at God's plan and the identity of Christ.

Look Deeper

Open your Bible and **read Psalm 110** at least once.

1. What do you learn about each "Lord" in the text—LORD and Lord?

2. In light of how the Lords are revealed in this passage, what does this teach us about humanity?

In Psalm 110, **the Holy Spirit cracks open a window for David to eavesdrop on a conversation between the Lord**—God's personal covenant name—and

David's Lord, a title that translates to Adonai and that the New Testament identifies as Jesus.[72]

From David's perspective, he knew this "Lord" was the promised Messiah from 2 Samuel 7, the one God said would come through his family line. But David didn't yet know the full picture of what the Messiah's rule—or the Messiah Himself—would look like. One day we'll get to have coffee with (or tea if you are one of those non-coffee drinkers I can't relate to) and ask David whether he only heard this divine conversation or actually saw something of it. Either way, it's powerful to imagine David receiving and recording a direct dialogue between God the Father and Jesus.

Since it's rare to "eavesdrop" on a conversation between God and Jesus (remember our study in Psalm 2 where we got to do the same!), it makes sense to assume God wanted us to pay attention. What He reveals here is all about the identity and role of Jesus.

David writes that God tells the Messiah, "Sit at my right hand," promising that His enemies will be placed under His authority (Psalm 110:1). Then comes this beautiful picture of the gospel's reach: God tells Jesus He will "extend [Jesus'] mighty scepter from Zion" (verse 2). The conversation keeps going as **God describes the Messiah's people—His "troops"—as willing and ready on the day of battle**. These people are described with imagery full of life and holiness: adorned in "holy splendor," coming "like dew from the morning's womb" (verse 3). It's a picture of strength and vitality.

Then God gives Jesus a title that would have stunned ancient readers: a priest "in the order of Melchizedek" (verse 4). Melchizedek shows up back in Genesis 14, and while we won't take a full detour today (trying to stay in the twenty-minute range!), the point is that this priesthood points to an *eternal* reign. The Messiah won't just be a king—He will be a priest forever.

72 "What Is the Meaning of Adonai?" GotQuestions, accessed March 24, 2026, https://www.gotquestions.org/meaning-of-Adonai.html.

The psalm closes with a scene of the Messiah entering battle, conquering kings, and executing justice among the nations. The final image is the Messiah pausing to drink and lifting His head high—an uncertain but likely symbolic picture of renewed strength and victorious rule.

What Does the Scripture Mean?

1. Some commentators see Psalm 110 as referring to Jesus' spiritual victory and reign rather than an actual real battle—such as Armageddon. If this is so, what might the **spiritual implications mean of His enemies being a footstool** under His feet (verse 1)? What might the spiritual implications mean of His troops/people being willing and ready on the day of battle (verse 3)?

2. What is the significance of the word "willing," or the phrase "offer themselves freely" (ESV), being included in verse 3? What does that mean for God's people today?

3. Why might God have wanted David and us to know that He "has sworn and will not change his mind" on the Messiah's reign and priesthood (verse 4)?

Connect to the Heart of Jesus

Truly, we could spend days in the New Testament passages that interpret Psalm 110. Instead, we will focus on one by Jesus Himself. Like Psalm 95, we are going to take the opportunity to use the Bible's own commentary to give meaning to the passage.

While the Pharisees were gathered together, Jesus asked them,
"What do you think about the Messiah? Whose son is he?"
"The son of David," they replied.
He said to them, "How is it then that David,
speaking by the Spirit, calls him 'Lord'? For he says,
"'The Lord said to my Lord: "Sit at my right hand
until I put your enemies under your feet."'
If then David calls him 'Lord,' how can he be his son?"

No one could say a word in reply, and from that day on no one dared to ask him any more questions.

(MATTHEW 22:41–46)

1. How does Jesus use leading questions in this passage to point to the meaning of Psalm 110?

2. What is Jesus hoping the Pharisees will see about who David is describing?

3. How and why did the Pharisees most likely respond the way they did (verse 46)?

Apply & Take Action

1. Does my heart feel "willing" or ready to offer myself freely to whatever the Lord is calling me to do?

2. In light of what I learned, why do you think this passage is quoted most in the New Testament?

3. When I look at my choices, priorities, and attitudes, do they show a life submitted to Jesus as King? What might God want me to change?

Pray and ask God to help you apply His truth to your life.

BIBLE BITES for PSALM 110

1. Peter quotes Psalm 110 on Pentecost, showing that David prophesied on the deity of Jesus (Acts 2:34–35).

2. **Paul refers to Psalm 110 in 1 Corinthians 15:25** to highlight the rule of Jesus.

3. Hebrews 1:13 quotes Psalm 110 as a statement that Jesus is superior over the angels.

STUDY 34

The Rejected Stone That Saves

Psalm 118

KEY VERSE

The stone the builders rejected has become the cornerstone.

(VERSE 22)

Pause . . . pray . . . and ask God for help in today's study.

Capturing the profound depth of Psalm 118 in just twenty minutes is undeniably challenging. My husband spent an entire month in Psalm 118 and journaled forty-two pages (and should I mention he only recently started journaling in the past two years?). I couldn't write this study without a heartfelt plea for you to at some point go deeper and linger longer in this psalm. On the flip side, like all the psalms, every line and phrase holds weight and meaning. If you only take one lesson or verse from this psalm, I believe your life can be changed.

Look Deeper

Open your Bible and **read Psalm 118** at least once.

1. What attributes of God does the author highlight in this psalm?

2. What challenges is the author facing?

The psalm opens with a call to praise: "Give thanks to the LORD, for he is good; his love endures forever." That word "love" is the Hebrew hesed that we explored earlier in our studies—God's loyal, covenant-keeping, never-letting-go kind of love. The psalmist then invites everyone—Israel, the house of Aaron, and even "those who fear the LORD" (which includes all of us who follow Him)—to join in declaring that this love truly lasts forever (verse 4).

Charles Spurgeon once noted that even the word "endures" doesn't fully capture how deep God's hesed really is. He said it's better understood as "his mercy endures forever." A love with no starting point and no ending point.[73]

---

73 David Guzik, "Psalm 118—the Chief Cornerstone," Enduring Word Bible Commentary, Enduring Word, accessed March 24, 2026, https://enduringword.com/bible-commentary/psalm-118.

Right after this call to praise, the psalmist gets honest: He's been "hard pressed" (verse 5). (Relatable, isn't it!) **Life has been crushing him, but he cried out—and God answered.** Then he does something we've seen in other psalms we have studied: He starts preaching truth to his own heart. "The LORD is with me; I will not be afraid. What can mere mortals do to me?" (verse 6) And as if he needs to hear it one more time (don't we all?), he repeats it: "The LORD is with me" (verse 7).

From there, he declares his trust in God (verses 8–9) and remembers the many ways God has brought him victory. But then comes a surprising turn—he admits that some of his struggle wasn't just from enemies; it was actually discipline from God (verse 18). In other words, **he didn't only need saving from others—he also needed saving from himself.**

And how does he respond? With gratitude:

I will give you thanks, for you answered me;
you have become my salvation.

(VERSE 21)

Then the psalm shifts again into something even more profound. The writer declares: "The stone the builders rejected has become the cornerstone" (verse 22). We'll later learn this is a prophetic statement pointing to Jesus, but even here, the psalmist recognizes God's ability to turn rejection into foundation, loss into strength. He follows it with praise, rejoicing, and a prayer for continued rescue (verse 25).

The psalm ends where it began—by thanking the Lord for His goodness and His hesed—love (verse 29). It's like the author is reminding us that no matter what we walk through—pressure, discipline, victory, confusion—**God's steadfast love is the beginning, the middle, and the end of our story.** It sustains us in everything we face.

What Does the Scripture Mean?

1. What might it mean that God brought the author into a "spacious place" after being "hard pressed" (verse 5)?

2. How do we reconcile the author's statement, "What can mere mortals do to me?" (verse 6) with the truth that man can hurt us? What deeper meaning might his statement hold?

3. Do verses 8–9 mean to not trust at all in humans or leaders? Why or why not?

4. What are the "gates of the righteous" (verse 19)?

5. In the context of the psalms and God's people, what might the meaning be for the "stone the builders rejected has become the cornerstone" (verse 22)?

Connect to the Heart of Jesus

Bible scholars differ on whether Psalm 118 points to Jesus in its entirety or only in certain verses. But what's undeniable is that Jesus quotes verse 22—"The stone the builders rejected has become the cornerstone"—and applies it directly to His own identity.

In Mark 12, Jesus tells a parable about wicked tenants who kill the vineyard owner's son. It's a vivid picture of Israel's long history of rejecting God's messengers—and ultimately rejecting Jesus, the Son. At the end of the parable, Jesus looks at the religious leaders and says:

"Haven't you read this passage of Scripture:
'The stone the builders rejected has become the cornerstone;
the Lord has done this, and it is marvelous in our eyes'?"

(MARK 12:10–11)

Here, Jesus is quoting Psalm 118—and also echoing Isaiah 28:16, where God says He is laying down a precious, tested cornerstone in Zion, a sure foundation for all who trust in Him. This "precious stone" is Jesus, the one the builders rejected for our sake.

In construction, the cornerstone is the main stone that sets the direction for the entire structure. Everything else aligns with it. Paul takes this imagery even further in Ephesians 2. We are no longer outsiders, he says, but members of God's household—"built on the foundation of the apostles and prophets, with Christ Jesus himself as the chief cornerstone" (Ephesians 2:20). In Him, we're being built together into a place where God Himself dwells by His Spirit.

So Jesus—rejected, crucified, raised—is the cornerstone and the foundation of our salvation.

Psalm 118 also has a deep historical backdrop. It's part of the *Hallel*, a collection of praise psalms that Israel has sung for centuries, especially during Passover.[74] These psalms were sung before the Passover lamb was sacrificed and later became part of the Passover meal itself.

In Matthew 26:30, we're told that after Jesus celebrated the Passover with His disciples, "they sang a hymn" (NLT). Many scholars believe this hymn would likely have been from the Hallel—meaning **Jesus' last recorded song with others before going to the cross may very well have been Psalm 118**. Amazing.

74 Menachem Posner, "What Is Hallel?" Chabad, accessed March 24, 2026, www.chabad.org/library/article_cdo/aid/4181720/jewish/What-Is-Hallel.htm.

Even if it wasn't His final song, it's breathtaking to imagine Jesus singing these words—knowing full well that He was the cornerstone, the rejected stone who would become the foundation, and that these ancient words would be fulfilled through His victory over death.

Apply & Take Action

1. How have I seen God's goodness and demonstration of His hesed (love) this week, and how can I thank Him?

2. How might I be trusting in humans or leaders more than the Lord?

3. Is there any way I see that the Lord might be chastening or disciplining me now? How can I respond with humility and repentance?

Pray and ask God to help you apply His truth to your life.

BIBLE BITES for PSALM 118

1. Martin Luther considered Psalm 118 his "beloved psalm," one of great comfort and strength.[75]

2. Numerous references point to Psalm 118 as the center of the Bible, but technically this is incorrect, and **Psalm 117 would be the center chapter.**

3. Scholars believe Ezra 3:10–11 indicates that Psalm 118 was sung at the finishing of the temple foundation.

75 Stephen Nichols, "242. Luther on Psalm 118," Ligonier Ministries, October 19, 2022, https://learn.ligonier.org/podcasts/5-minutes-in-church-history-with-stephen-nichols/242-luther-on-psalm-118.

STUDY 35

Eyes Up

Psalm 121

KEY VERSE

My help comes from the LORD,
the Maker of heaven and earth.

(VERSE 2)

Pause . . . pray . . . and ask God for help in today's study.

We are diving into a Psalm of Ascent today, and it is worth reading a thorough description of what these psalms are: "The Songs of Ascent are a special group of psalms comprising Psalms 120–134. They are also called Pilgrim Songs. . . . The city of Jerusalem is situated on a high hill. Jews traveling to Jerusalem for one of the three main annual Jewish festivals traditionally sang these songs on the 'ascent' or the uphill road to the city. Each of the psalms in this collection begins with the title 'A Song of Ascents.' While perhaps they were not originally composed for this purpose, these psalms were later grouped together for use in traveling toward Jerusalem for the yearly Jewish festivals."[76]

And even though God's presence is no longer tied to a single building, the Psalms of Ascent still give us a picture of what our own spiritual journey looks like. We're all "on the way" somewhere—navigating work, relationships, transitions, disappointments, and joys. **These psalms remind us that faith isn't a static belief system; it's a journey with God, one step at a time.**

Look Deeper

Open your Bible and read Psalm 121 at least once.

1. What names and characteristics are attributed to God in this psalm?

2. What is the significance of the psalmist lifting his eyes up? Given the context of the psalms, what might have led him to feel the need to lift his eyes up?

76 "What are the Songs of Ascent?" GotQuestions, accessed March 24, 2026, www.gotquestions.org/Songs-of-Ascent.html.

What Does the Scripture Mean?

In the same way David looked at the skies and saw evidence of God's power in Psalm 8, the writer of Psalm 121 looks at the mountains and is reminded of who God is. The hills aren't just scenery on the road—they point him to the Creator, and to the confidence that his help comes from the Lord.

It helps to remember what this journey actually looked like. This pilgrim didn't have a car, GPS, or a perfectly planned route—and definitely no coffee stop along the way. Traveling to Jerusalem meant walking long distances through rough terrain, often exposed to danger. History and geography both tell us these journeys could be exhausting and risky.[77] **The Psalms of Ascent weren't written from a place of comfort, but from the reality of people putting one foot in front of the other on a difficult journey.**

As the psalm continues, there may be a shift in narrator—possibly to a priest or spiritual guide walking alongside the pilgrim. This voice speaks reassurance into the fear: *God never sleeps.*

He will not let your foot slip—
he who watches over you will not slumber;
indeed, he who watches over Israel
will neither slumber nor sleep.

(VERSES 3–4)

---

77 Megan Sauter, "3 Pilgrimage Paths from Galilee to Jerusalem," Biblical Archaeology Society, January 25, 2026, www.biblicalarchaeology.org/daily/biblical-topics/new-testament/3-pilgrimage-paths-from-galilee-to-jerusalem; "Travel," Bible Gateway, accessed March 24, 2026, www.biblegateway.com/resources/encyclopedia-of-the-bible/Travel.

That matters, because the risks were constant—day and night. During the day, the Middle Eastern sun could be brutal, draining strength and focus. Yet the psalm says God would be a "shade" (and not in our modern-day negative sense) offering protection and relief (verse 5). At night, when travel brought new fears—darkness, isolation, and uncertainty—the pilgrim is reminded that even then, God is still watching: "The sun shall not strike you by day, nor the moon by night" (verse 6 ESV).

The psalm closes with a powerful promise. God will guard the pilgrim from all harm—or all evil. Watching over every part of life, every "coming and going" on this pilgrim's journey, God would watch over him (verse 8).

What Does the Scripture Mean?

1. What does it mean that God is not just the creator of earth, but also of heaven (verse 2)?

2. How does this psalm portray God's attentiveness when compared to human watchfulness?

3. Do you think the promises in this psalm are absolute, poetic, circumstantial, or something else?

4. How is this physical journey symbolic of our spiritual journey?

Connect to the Heart of Jesus

Jesus affirms what Psalm 121 assumes—that **creation can point us to God's care.** As we referenced in some earlier studies, in His teaching, Jesus repeatedly draws our attention to the world around us, reminding us that if God faithfully cares for the birds, the flowers, and even the grass, how much more will He care for us (Matthew 6:26–30). **Creation isn't meant to distract us; it's meant to reorient us**—to lift our eyes from anxiety to trust.

While our lives may not involve a physical pilgrimage to Jerusalem, we are still on a journey. And, like the psalmist, our eyes often need to be lifted—away from our circumstances, our problems, and yes, even (maybe especially at times) our phones. It's striking how modern life trains us to do the opposite of Psalm 121: Instead of looking up, we are constantly looking down. Yet **Jesus invites us, just as the psalm does, to lift our eyes—to see beyond what's immediately in front of us and remember that our help comes from the Lord,** the One who watches over us with constant, attentive care. Unlike the pilgrim in Psalm 121, we no longer journey through perilous roads to encounter God's presence—His presence is now constantly with us through Christ.

We're called to fix our eyes on Jesus in every journey of life:

Let us run with perseverance the race marked out for us,
fixing our eyes on Jesus, the pioneer and perfecter of faith.

(HEBREWS 12:1–2)

Apply & Take Action

1. If I could describe my spiritual journey as a point along a pilgrimage, where would I place myself right now? What does that part of the journey look like for me?

2. Where do my eyes most often look for help? What would it look like to lift my spiritual eyes to Jesus more?

3. Psalm 121:8 talks about God watching over our "coming and going." How can this assurance shape my daily routines, priorities, or decisions in practical ways?

4. How can I support or encourage someone else who may be on a treacherous part of their own spiritual journey?

Pray and ask God to help you apply His truth to your life.

BIBLE BITES for PSALM 121

1. Not as noticeable at first glance, **Psalm 121 is written in parallelism,** each line reinforcing the previous line.

2. Psalm 121 has been suggested by a variety of writers and scholars to be the "Traveler's Psalm."[78]

3. Charles Spurgeon named Psalm 21 "A Song of Degrees."[79]

78 "Psalm—121:1–8," Bibleocity, accessed March 24, 2026, www.bibleocity.com/Psalm/121.

79 Charles Spurgeon, "Psalm 121," Spurgeon Archive, accessed March 24, 2026, https://archive.spurgeon.org/treasury/ps121.php.

STUDY 36

Built by God, Not by Hands

Psalm 127

KEY VERSE

In vain you rise early and stay up late,

toiling for food to eat—for he grants sleep to those he loves.

(VERSE 2)

Pause . . . pray . . . and ask God for help in today's study.

As I began studying Psalm 127 some time ago, I skipped over the introduction and the author. But as I read our theme verse, one word stood out to me: vain.

That word immediately brought Ecclesiastes to mind. Ecclesiastes is essentially a reflection on how life is meaningless—the original word used is *hevel* in Hebrew, like a vapor—when it's lived apart from God.[80]

As I sat with that thought, I wondered if Solomon might have written this psalm. And then, almost ironically, I finally noticed the title: a psalm "of Solomon." While **some commentators think it was possibly written by David for Solomon, many attribute it to Solomon,** and I think we will find it sounds most like his voice.

I share this as a simple reminder: God's Word is seamless, even when we aren't aware of the connections. Scripture doesn't contradict itself—it echoes, builds, and weaves together one unified truth. I hope you are also realizing that as we connect the psalms to Jesus and the New Testament.

Look Deeper

Open your Bible and read Psalm 127 at least once.

1. What actions in this psalm are attributed directly to God?

2. How is human striving shown specifically in this psalm and compared to God's control?

80 "Hevel (Remastered)," BibleProject, accessed March 6, 2026, https://bibleproject.com/podcasts/ecclesiastes-part-1-hevel/.

Psalm 127 is one of only two psalms written by King Solomon (the other is Psalm 72). Solomon was the son of King David.

God gave Solomon wisdom and very great insight, and a breadth of understanding as measureless as the sand on the seashore. Solomon's wisdom was greater than the wisdom of all the people of the East, and greater than all the wisdom of Egypt. He was wiser than anyone else.

(1 KINGS 4:29–31)

And yet later in life, in the book of Ecclesiastes, Solomon looks back and finds every pursuit apart from glorifying God is empty and meaningless. That reflection also becomes the heartbeat of Psalm 127.

The psalm opens with a weighty declaration: "Unless the LORD builds the house, the builders labor in vain" (verse 1). This was not a theoretical statement for Solomon. He had been personally commissioned to build a house of immense significance—the house of the Lord, the temple. David had long desired to build it himself, but God made it clear that the task would belong to his son:

"'Solomon your son is the one who will build my house and my courts, for I have chosen him to be my son, and I will be his father.'"

(1 CHRONICLES 28:6)

Both David and Solomon knew firsthand what it meant to build only at God's direction. They believed (though not always lived) the truth that **human effort, no matter how skilled or sincere, is empty unless it is grounded in God's calling.** Furthermore, as kings who saw a lot of battles and wars, Solomon and his father experienced the truth asserted in the second part of the verse: "Unless the LORD watches over the city, the guards stand watch in vain."

Solomon pushes this even further in verse 2: "In vain you rise early and stay up late, toiling for food to eat—for he grants sleep to those he loves." It echoes what he also writes in Ecclesiastes:

> *What do people get for all the toil and anxious striving with which they labor under the sun? . . . Even at night their minds do not rest.*
>
> (ECCLESIASTES 2:22–23)

Solomon isn't saying, "Don't work hard." He's saying, "Don't give your life to work God never assigned you." **When our striving isn't rooted in God's calling, it produces anxiety, exhaustion, and restless nights—not fulfillment.**

In closing, Solomon shares the blessing and honor of having children, which (again), given the historical context, carries a sad note as the only recorded and named son of Solomon—is Rehoboam, who caused the kingdom to split in two.

What Does the Scripture Mean?

1. What does it mean to have the Lord be the One to build and watch, in light of our own role in our work and planning?

2. How should we interpret "He grants sleep to those he loves" (Psalm 127:2)? Is this about rest, trust, provision, or all three?

3. Why does the psalm move from **work and cities** to **children and family,** and what does it mean to view children as a "heritage" or "reward" from the Lord (verse 3)?

Connect to the Heart of Jesus

Jesus deepens the theme of Psalm 127—the truth that apart from God, all human effort is ultimately vain—when He teaches His disciples:

"I am the vine; you are the branches.
If you remain in me and I in you,
you will bear much fruit;
apart from me you can do nothing."

(JOHN 15:5)

Apart from remaining in Christ—abiding in His presence, guidance, and power—our efforts cannot produce anything that truly glorifies God or reflects the character of the Spirit. Whereas Psalm 127 speaks of the futility of laboring in vain without God, Jesus broadens the principle: **Everything in life—work, relationships, spiritual practice, and even daily tasks—is ultimately unfruitful unless it is rooted in Him**. His message does not soften the psalm; it intensifies it.

Jesus also deepens Solomon's affirmation of children. Psalm 127 calls children a "heritage" and a blessing from the Lord (verse 3). Jesus goes further, welcoming children Himself and highlighting their qualities as a model for His followers:

> *He called a little child to him, and placed the child among them. And he said: "Truly I tell you, unless you change and become like little children, you will never enter the kingdom of heaven. Therefore, whoever takes the lowly position of this child is the greatest in the kingdom of heaven. And whoever welcomes one such child in my name welcomes me."*
>
> (MATTHEW 18:2–5)

Children are naturally humble, teachable, and dependent—qualities Jesus calls His disciples to possess. In doing so, He shows that blessing is not only in receiving children but also in adopting their disposition of trust and openness before God.

In sum, Jesus both confirms and intensifies Psalm 127: Our labor, relationships, and fruitfulness are in vain apart from Him, and children exemplify the humble, dependent posture we are called to cultivate as we remain in the Lord.

Apply & Take Action

1. Am I struggling with any stress or lack of sleep? How might this psalm be revealing the root of it?

2. Is there anything I am building, watching for, working for, or cultivating in life apart from Him—whether in relationships, work, ministry, family life, and so on? How can I surrender it to the Lord?

3. How does viewing children as a "heritage from the LORD" (Psalm 127:3) affect the way I relate to children, family, or younger generations? In what ways can I or am I investing in raising or mentoring others with intentionality, like "arrows in the hands of a warrior" (verse 4)?

Pray and ask God to help you apply His truth to your life.

BIBLE BITES for PSALM 127

1. There is a collection of **eighteen psalms known as the "Psalms of Solomon,"** but they were written many years after his death and are not attributed to him by scholars.[81]

2. The phrase "those he loves" in verse 2 has the **same root word of the name Jedidiah,** the first name given to Solomon by God in 2 Samuel 12:25, which means "Beloved of the Lord" in Hebrew.

3. Psalm 127 is also part of the Psalms of Ascents, which are discussed in detail in study 35.

81 "What Are the Psalms of Solomon?" GotQuestions, accessed March 24, 2026, www.gotquestions .org/Psalms-of-Solomon.html.

STUDY 37

Be Still, My Soul

Psalm 131

KEY VERSE

But I have calmed and quieted myself.

(VERSE 2)

Pause . . . pray . . . and ask God for help in today's study.

Charles Spurgeon once said of Psalm 131, "It is one of the shortest psalms to read, but one of the longest to learn."[82] And his sentiment feels especially true for us. This psalm describes a calm and quiet soul—something that can feel almost out of reach in our generation. Compared to Spurgeon's world in the 1800s, we live with nonstop technology, endless news cycles, and constant opinions, all the time.

82 Charles Spurgeon, "Psalm 131," Spurgeon Archive, accessed March 24, 2026, https://archive.spurgeon.org/treasury/ps131.php.

And while a calm and quiet soul might feel impossible, the ancient—but still living—words of Psalm 131 tell a different story. Regardless of our modern world and all its noise, **Psalm 131 teaches us that a calm and quiet soul isn't just a feel-good sentiment—it's actually possible.**

Look Deeper

Open your Bible and read Psalm 131 at least once.

1. What do the psalmist's declarations—and the way he looks to God—teach us about God's character?

2. What does the way the psalmist approaches God teach us about humanity?

We find ourselves journeying through another Psalm of Ascent, written by David. As David sets his mind and heart toward worship, he makes a striking declaration: "My heart is not proud, LORD, my eyes are not haughty" (verse 1). That kind of humility is remarkable, especially in the ancient Mediterranean world, where kings and nations were most often defined by pride and self-promotion.

David uses the Hebrew word *leb* for "heart," a word that points to the very center of a person—the will, the intellect, and the emotions.[83] In other words, David is holding nothing back. His humility isn't surface-level or performative; it's a posture of his whole being.

Flowing out of that humility, David makes a deliberate choice: "I do not concern myself with great matters or things too wonderful for me" (verse 1). And that's astonishing when you remember David is a king—the highest authority among God's people apart from the high priest. Yet David resolves to stay present and faithful to what God has actually entrusted to him. He refuses to meddle in ideas, outcomes, responsibilities, ministries, or circumstances that God has not given him the calling or power to carry.

Then verse 2 begins with a turning point, a conjunction word: "But." David reveals the antidote to pride and haughtiness: "But I have calmed and quieted myself; I am like a weaned child with its mother; like a weaned child I am content" (verse 2). Instead of reaching for greater matters beyond his calling, David chooses to calm and quiet his soul. He embraces the humility of being like a child with his mother.

Unlike a nursing infant—constantly crying out for immediate satisfaction—a weaned child is content, not with what the mother gives, but with her presence.

David finishes by encouraging God's people to put their hope in God.

---

83 Strong's Hebrew 3820, לֵב (leb): heart, hearts, mind.

What Does the Scripture Mean?

1. Why does the psalmist address pride before rest? How specifically does pride impede rest?

2. What does it mean to "hope in the LORD" (verse 3) in light of the psalmist's posture of humility?

3. What is the significance of David exhorting God's people to put their hope in both now and forevermore?

Connect to the Heart of Jesus

One of the wonders of the incarnation is the humility with which Jesus entered the world. He didn't arrive with power and status, but in a position even lower than a weaned child—as a nursing infant, completely dependent on others. And that humility didn't disappear as He grew older. As an adult, **Jesus willingly embraced the real physical limitations of being human.** He experienced hunger (Mark 11:12), thirst (John 19:28), and exhaustion (John 4:6).

But Jesus' humility wasn't only physical—it was also deeply spiritual and relational. He didn't say yes to every relationship (Luke 6:13). He didn't respond to every ministry opportunity (Luke 4:43). He refused to act independently of the Father (John 5:30). Even His own disciples seemed confused by this, especially when Jesus stepped away from the crowds to spend time alone in prayer (Mark 1:35–37).

In all of this, Jesus willingly subjected Himself to human limitations—not out of weakness, but out of humility. He embodied what David declared long ago: We can't—and shouldn't try to—do it all. **We're not meant to take on things God hasn't opened the door for.** Jesus said no because of physical limits, yes—but also because of spiritual discernment. As a man, He was deeply committed to doing only what the Father had called Him to do.

Jesus said,

"Very truly I tell you, the Son can do nothing by himself;
he can do only what he sees his Father doing,
because whatever the Father does the Son also does."

(JOHN 5:19)

Though Jesus took on the weight and sins of the world—and He knew more news and opinions than our incessant scrolling gives us access to information—He walked in peace, and He was the peace He offered to us:

"Peace I leave with you; my peace I give you."

(JOHN 14:27)

Jesus lived out the path to a calm and quiet soul in a loud and restless world—choosing humility and showing us that real peace comes from looking to Him.

Apply & Take Action

1. What matters or things have I been carrying that God never asked me to carry, and why?

2. What are some practical steps God might be asking me to take to humble myself (say no, apologize, take a step back, etc.)?

3. What would it look like to accept my God-given limits instead of resisting them?

4. What would it look like to intentionally calm and quiet myself this week?

5. What does hoping in the Lord look like in my current season of life?

Pray and ask God to help you apply His truth to your life.

BIBLE BITES for PSALM 131

1. Two common suggestions for the context of Psalm 131 are either when Saul hunted David, or when Michal, David's wife, despised him for dancing before the ark of the covenant.

2. The phrase "put your hope in" found in verse 3 is an active verb, not passive.

3. Psalm 131 is essentially tied for second place with Psalm 133 and 134 for the shortest psalm of the Bible, behind Psalm 117.

STUDY 38

A Guard for Our Words and Heart

Psalm 141

KEY VERSE

But my eyes are fixed on you, Sovereign LORD.

(VERSE 8)

Pause . . . pray . . . and ask God for help in today's study.

Psalm 141 is packed with so many nuggets of wisdom and points—it's one of those passages where almost every verse could have been our theme verse. At the same time, if you read it quickly, it can feel a little scattered. The themes shift, the tone changes, and it's not immediately obvious what thread is holding it all together.

That's actually part of what makes this psalm so relatable. While Scripture's authority and the Spirit's inspiration are our foundation, it's helpful to remember that the **psalms sometimes read like personal journal entries.** They capture real moments—prayers spoken in tension, reflection, fear, resolve, and trust—sometimes all in the same stanza. Psalm 141 isn't a polished essay; it's another snapshot of a real person—David, again—trying to walk faithfully with God in the middle of pressure and uncertainty. And honestly, that's an experience many of us are probably well-acquainted with.

Look Deeper

Open your Bible and **read Psalm 141** at least once.

1. How does what David asks of God reveal who God is—His character, priorities, and the kind of relationship He invites us into?

2. What stands out to you about David's heart or other references to people in this passage?

In Psalm 141, as we have seen him do in so many of our other psalm studies, David opens with a picture of passionate prayer. He urgently asks God to hear him when he calls (verse 1), and he wants his prayer to rise to God "like incense" (verse 2). This is a beautiful foreshadowing of the New Testament image in Revelation 5:8, where the prayers of God's people are described the same way.

David also asks that the lifting of his hands be like "the evening sacrifice" (verse 2). The evening sacrifice—also called the "continual burnt offering"—was offered every single day, symbolizing ongoing devotion and the need for atonement.[84] His heart posture of seeking forgiveness and guidance to walk rightly becomes even clearer in verses 3–4, where David pleads for help with the areas he knows are vulnerable: his words, his heart, and his actions. He's not just worried about outside threats—he's asking God to protect him from becoming part of the evil around him.

And even though David wants nothing to do with "evildoers" (verse 4), he openly welcomes correction from a righteous person (verse 5). He describes that rebuke as "oil on [his] head"—a powerful image in Scripture that represents healing and refreshment (verse 5). David receives the correction with a humble and teachable heart. What a remarkable picture in light of an individualistic culture—even aspects that have seeped into the church—where we have overused and misused the phrase *Do not judge*. And he makes it clear that accepting correction doesn't mean aligning with evil—his prayers remain firmly against the actions of the wicked (verses 5–7).

With all this injustice and brokenness swirling around him, David closes this section with clarity and resolve: "But my eyes are fixed on you, Sovereign LORD" (verse 8). Instead of being consumed by what's going wrong, he looks to God as his refuge and protector. He asks God to preserve his life, keep him safe from traps, and ultimately bring justice.

---

84 "The Evening Sacrifice," Bible Hub, accessed March 24, 2026, https://biblehub.com/topical/t/the_evening_sacrifice.htm.

What Does the Scripture Mean?

1. Why do you think the psalm moves between confession, moral resolution, and pleadings?

2. What does this psalm suggest about the connection between temptation, speech, and behavior?

3. What does it look like to eat of the "delicacies" of the wicked in a real, practical sense (verse 4)?

4. What does David believe God has the power to control—externally and internally?

Connect to the Heart of Jesus

In the incarnation, we see something truly remarkable: Jesus not only models what it looks like to pray earnestly—like David does in this psalm—He also becomes the very reason we're able to draw near to God at all. **Jesus prays with honesty and urgency, and at the same time,** He opens the door for us to approach the Father with that same kind of freedom and confidence.

Because of that, it might be tempting to read quickly past verse 3—"Set a guard over my mouth, LORD; keep watch over the door of my lips"—but this line deserves our attention as it represents a repetitive theme in Scripture. **The Bible talks about the tongue, the mouth, and our speech roughly 130 times,** and Jesus returns to this topic again and again. One of His most revealing statements reads:

"For the mouth speaks what the heart is full of."

(MATTHEW 12:34)

In other words, our words aren't just careless sounds we make—they're diagnostic of our heart condition and reveal what's really going on inside us.

David asks God to guard his mouth, but he doesn't stop there. He immediately connects his words to his inner life: "Do not let my heart be drawn to what is evil so that I take part in wicked deeds" (Psalm 141:4). David recognizes a progression we still experience today—**what captures the heart eventually shapes our words, and our words, in turn, shape our actions.** Jesus continues this thread of teaching throughout His ministry.

That's why it's important to rethink the common cultural picture of Jesus as simply a "nice guy." While Jesus is compassionate and gentle, He also regularly rebukes and corrects—not only the religious leaders (Matthew 23:27–28; Mark 7:6–9), but even His own disciples (Matthew 16:21–23; Mark 4:40). Yet Jesus' correction is never driven by irritation or ego. It's always rooted in love and a desire for people to turn back to God. He meant it to be, as David suggests, like oil on the head.

We see this most clearly in Jesus' grief over Jerusalem:

> *"How often I have longed to gather your children together, as a hen gathers her chicks under her wings, and you were not willing."*
>
> (LUKE 13:34)

Jesus becomes the ultimate picture of the "righteous man" David depicts that rebukes and corrects, and who does it out of kindness (Psalm 141:5).

Apply & Take Action

1. How do my words reflect my heart? Is there any way I need to ask God to set a guard over my mouth today?

2. How do I or how have I received correction or rebuke from others?

3. Is there anyone I need to correct or rebuke in the spirit of kindness this week?

4. What does it look like practically to fix my eyes on God today?

Pray and ask God to help you apply His truth to your life.

BIBLE BITES for PSALM 141

1. The first person anointed with oil in the Bible was Aaron, the brother of Moses, as part of the consecration of his priesthood (Exodus 29:7).

2. **David was first anointed with oil by the prophet Samuel** to signify his being chosen as king by God (1 Samuel 16).

3. The book of James instructs elders to pray over and anoint sick people with oil (James 5:14–16).

STUDY 39

A Hope Beyond Ourselves

Psalm 143

KEY VERSE

Do not bring your servant into judgment,
for no one living is righteous before you.

(VERSE 2)

Pause . . . pray . . . and ask God for help in today's study.

Psalm 143 is another one of those psalms that feels like it's moving in a lot of directions at once. There are several themes woven through it, but beneath them all runs a steady undercurrent of personal pleading and prayer. **David is once again raw, urgent, and intensely personal.**

What's striking is just how bold David is. His pleas are passionate—almost confrontational at times. In fact, pastor John Piper once preached a sermon on this psalm titled "How to Argue with God."[85] And that title fits. David isn't holding back. He's pressing in, reasoning with God, and laying out his case with hunger and desperation.

Yet all of David's bold requests rest on one striking confession, our key verse of the psalm:

Do not bring your servant into judgment,
for no one living is righteous before you.

(VERSE 2)

That raises an important question: How can David pray with such confidence, how can he plead so boldly, even argue before a holy and perfect God, while openly admitting that no one is righteous before Him?

The answer, I believe, takes us to the very foundation of this psalm—and really, to the foundation of every psalm we have studied and all Scripture. **David's confidence is not rooted in his own righteousness, but in God's grace.** Psalm 143 ultimately drives us toward the same place every word of God leads us: the grace of God and the hope of the gospel.

Look Deeper

Open your Bible and read Psalm 143 at least once.

1. What assumptions about God's character allow David to pray with such urgency, honesty, and even boldness in Psalm 143?

85 John Piper, "How to Argue with God," Desiring God, August 25, 1980, www.desiringgod.org/messages/how-to-argue-with-god.

2. What do you learn about humanity in Psalm 143 when observing David's accusations of the enemy and also his own pleadings?

Distressed—again. We've walked through many psalms where David is under pressure, and at first glance this one feels familiar. He's once more being hunted by enemies, and he puts it in stark, almost physical terms: "He crushes me to the ground" (verse 3). He tells us his spirit is "faint," his heart "dismayed" (verse 4).

But what's striking in Psalm 143 is that David doesn't just point outward at his enemies; he also looks inward. In the middle of pleading for rescue, he makes a stunning confession: "Do not bring your servant into judgment, for no one living is righteous before you" (verse 2). In other words, David knows that if this situation were about his moral résumé, he'd have no case. No one, he says—including himself—can stand before God on the basis of personal righteousness.

That's why David argues his case the way he does. He doesn't appeal to his own goodness, effort, or faithfulness. Instead, he anchors everything in who God is: "In your faithfulness and righteousness come to my relief" (verse 1). **David knows that his only hope isn't found in his character, but in God's.** And as we've seen him do again and again in Psalms, he strengthens his present faith by remembering God's past works—meditating on what God has done so he can trust Him for what he's doing now (verse 5).

After pleading for deliverance from his enemies, David's prayer goes even deeper than circumstantial relief. Rescue isn't enough. He longs for spiritual direction and heart transformation: "Show me the way I should go" (verse 8) and "Teach me to do your will" (verse 10). This isn't just a prayer to get out of trouble; it's a prayer to be aligned with God's heart.

And David bookends the psalm with more appeal to God's character; for His "name's sake" does David appeal to God to preserve his life (verse 11), and because of His "unfailing love" does David plead to God to bring justice on his enemies (verse 12).

And in a beautiful, resounding ending, David declares his identity in spite of the hardships that surround him: "I am your servant" (verse 12).

What Does the Scripture Mean?

1. Why did David specifically appeal to God's faithfulness and righteousness when he called out to Him (verse 1)?

2. From what you know of David's life and biblical history prior to David's life, **what are some of the works he might have meditated upon** as he considered what God had done (verse 5)?

3. What does the imagery in verse 6 mean: "I spread out my hands to you; I thirst for you like a parched land"? What images or emotions is David hoping to conjure?

4. What does it mean to "let the morning bring me word of your unfailing love" (verse 8)? What is the significance of it being the morning?

Connect to the Heart of Jesus

Romans 3:20, while not a direct quote, is seen by many as echoing Psalm 143:2—"Do not bring your servant into judgment, for no one living is righteous before you."

Paul tells us:

Therefore no one will be declared righteous in God's sight by the works of the law; rather, through the law we become conscious of our sin.

(ROMANS 3:20)

We saw David spend much of Psalm 143 lamenting the wickedness of his enemies—their attacks on him, opposition to God, and injustice. But as he reflects on their actions in light of God's law, something humbling happens: David doesn't just see their sin. He sees his own. The law doesn't simply expose what's wrong out there; it turns the spotlight inward. David becomes, in Paul's words, "conscious of [his] sin."

Paul continues:

But now apart from the law the righteousness of God has been made known, to which the Law and the Prophets testify.

(ROMANS 3:21)

David knew the goodness of the law, but he also knew its limits. He understood that no one, including him, could meet its demands. That's why his plea rests not on his own obedience, but on God's character. As he prays in verse 1, he appeals to God's faithfulness and righteousness. Not his own.

Once again, as we've seen so often in the psalms, David is standing on the edge of something bigger than he can fully see. He is reaching forward and foreshadowing the gospel. And Paul names it clearly:

This righteousness is given through faith in Jesus Christ to all who believe.

(ROMANS 3:22)

What a place to land as we near the end (second to last) of our study in the Psalms: the gospel; the righteousness of Jesus—freely given, fully sufficient, covering all who believe in Him.

Friends, we can read every psalm. We can study deeply, answer application questions thoughtfully and sound incredibly spiritual. **But if our faith is not in Jesus Christ to save us, then all of it—every lesson or reflection—is what Psalm 127 calls "vain."** (Remember that word used two times?)

The heartbeat of the psalms has always been this: They point us to the grace of God, and ultimately, they point us to Jesus.

Yes, the psalmists cry out for rescue from circumstances. But underneath it all, they knew they needed a greater rescue. David's enemies were real—but temporary. His soul was eternal.

Psalm 143, like the rest of the psalms, gives us permission to bring every raw detail of our lives before God. Nothing is too messy, too emotional, or too small for Him to care about. And yet, it lovingly points us beyond our circumstances to our deepest need: righteousness we cannot produce on our own.

David hoped in the righteousness of God—a righteousness that would one day be fully revealed in Jesus. **Jesus is the fulfillment of every longing, every promise, every cry in the Psalms.** And our response, beautiful but necessary: *believe.*

Apply & Take Action

1. What does it look like in my life and with my busy schedule to seek or live in the word of His unfailing love every morning or day (verse 8)?

2. In what ways do I need God to show me the way I should go in life (verse 8)? Am I seeking to learn and follow His will in every area of my life (verse 10)?

3. In what ways can I live more as a servant to God (verse 12) and put my life under His full authority?

Pray and ask God to help you apply His truth to your life.

BIBLE BITES for PSALM 143

1. **Psalm 143 is one of the Seven Penitential Psalms**—those that are seen as expressing deep sorrow and repentance.

2. Due to a slightly different numbering system, Psalm 143 is actually Psalm 142 in the Latin Vulgate.

3. Augustine suggested that this psalm was written during the period of the rebellion of David's son, Absalom.[86]

86 Augustine, "Exposition on Psalm 143," New Advent, accessed March 24, 2026, www.newadvent.org/fathers/1801143.htm.

STUDY 40

Praise Is the Last and Forever Lyric

Psalm 150

KEY VERSE

Let everything that has breath praise the Lord.

(VERSE 6)

Pause . . . pray . . . and ask God for help in today's study.

What a journey this has been. And here we are—at the end of our Psalms study. If you've made it this far, well done, friend!

The number forty carries deep biblical significance. God sent rain on the earth for forty days and nights during the flood (Genesis 7:4). Moses remained on the mountain for forty days and nights as God confirmed His covenant with him

(Exodus 24). Goliath stood and taunted Israel for forty days (1 Samuel 17). And Jesus fasted for forty days in the wilderness while being tested (Matthew 4).

Now, in our own way, we've walked a "forty" of our own—forty lessons through the Psalms. Roughly twenty minutes at a time, showing up with open hearts, trusting God to meet us there and do far more than we could ask or imagine.

It feels fitting to end our final study with the final psalm—and to find that its theme is praise. Psalm 150 is believed to have been written after the Babylonian exile, around the time the Second Temple was built, when circumstances were finally improving.

But let us also remember that **throughout the psalms, praise was never limited to good seasons alone**. The psalmists worshiped God in joy, grief, fear, and waiting.

So if our lives don't match the celebratory tone of today's study, we are still encouraged to praise. May God give us the strength to praise Him right where we are in Psalm 150 today.

Today's study will be unique in that it will have less content and more time for reflection.

Look Deeper

Open your Bible and read Psalm 150 at least once.

1. What does this psalm reveal about who God is and where He should be praised?

2. Who is called to praise God, and how?

Each of the five books of the psalms (we've worked through eight psalms in each book) ends with a doxology—a hymn or short declaration of praise. Psalm 150 serves as a clear, passionate call for all of creation to praise God.

Andrew Maclaren captures this well when he says of Psalm 150:

> The psalm is more than an artistic close of the psalter; it is a prophecy of the last result of the devout life, and, in its unclouded sunniness, as well as its universality, it proclaims the certain end of the weary years for the individual and for the world.[87]

With resounding emphasis, both the psalm and the entire book of Psalms conclude with this exhortation: "Let everything that has breath praise the LORD" (verse 6). **The psalmist calls every living being to praise its Creator**—and Scripture tells us that one day this will, without exception, be true: "'As surely as I live,' says the Lord, 'every knee will bow before me; every tongue will acknowledge God'" (Romans 14:11, quoting Isaiah 45:23).

Psalm 150, however, shows us something crucial: It is far better to praise God now—freely, joyfully, even with dancing (verse 4)—as people who have chosen Him than to wait for the day when praise is no longer a choice but an unavoidable reality.

---

87 David Guzik, "Psalm 150—Let All Things Praise the Lord," Enduring Word Bible Commentary, Enduring Word, accessed March 24, 2026, https://enduringword.com/bible-commentary/psalm-150.

What Does the Scripture Mean?

1. What might be the significance of being called to praise God in two specific places—"in his sanctuary" and "in his mighty heavens" (verse 1)?

2. Why is praise exhorted to be universal and communal rather than just personal in this psalm?

3. What are the two categories the psalm gives of what to praise God for (verse 2), and how might these be described in other terms?

4. What does it mean in this psalm when it encourages praise through musical instruments and dancing, rather than doctrine or words?

Connect to the Heart of Jesus

Mirroring the way the book of Psalms ends, the final book of the Bible—Revelation—gives us a glimpse of where all of this is headed. One day everything that has breath will praise the Lord:

> *Then I heard every creature in heaven and on earth and under the earth and on the sea, and all that is in them, saying: "To him who sits on the throne and to the Lamb be praise and honor and glory and power, for ever and ever!"*
>
> (REVELATION 5:13)

The scene surrounding these words might take our breath away. John describes a vision of "thousands upon thousands" of angels encircling God's throne, joined by the elders, all lifting their voices in worship. At the center stands Jesus—also there called "the Lamb"—receiving the praise that belongs to God alone (verses 11–12).

This helps us understand why Jesus taught us to pray, "Your will be done, on earth as it is in heaven" (Matthew 6:10). In other words, **let's bring the praise scene of heaven into our lives on earth today,** in whatever that looks like for our personality and setting.

So let it be that this exuberant, heaven-shaped praise comes not only from everything that has breath someday, but from those of us who love Him now—with every breath we have, right up until our final one. We've already seen that praise and thanksgiving are good for our souls (Psalm 92), and Psalm 150 carries that anthem to its climactic conclusion.

So whether you're quietly at home today, or you feel moved to sing loudly, pick up an instrument (tambourine anyone?), or even dance—let's praise the Lamb of God, Jesus, our Savior, with the lives and breath He's given us.

Apply & Take Action

1. What are some acts of power from God I have experienced in my life that I can praise Him for right now?

2. What are some of God's attributes—alongside His surpassing greatness—that I can praise Him for right now?

3. What can I praise God for in these past forty lessons? How have I been shaped or transformed by these psalms?

4. What would it look like for my **everyday, ordinary moments** to reflect worship, not just my "spiritual" ones?

5. What work do I want God to continue to do in my life as I apply these forty psalms to my life?

Pray and ask God to help you apply His truth to your life.

BIBLE BITES for PSALM 150

1. The word **"praise" is repeated thirteen times** in this short psalm.

2. Nine instruments are mentioned in this short psalm.

3. Verse 4—"praise him with timbrel and dancing"—is also reminiscent of the deliverance at the Red Sea when Miriam, Aaron's sister, led the women in worship "with timbrels and dancing" (Exodus 15:20).

Let God Multiply Your Moments

An Invitation for the Busy Woman Longing for More of God's Word

---

Between work deadlines, school pickups, laundry piles, and endless responsibilities, many women wonder: *Can God really meet me in the little time I have?* Through this study of forty psalms, you'll discover that He can. Even twenty minutes with God's Word can renew your heart. The Psalms speak to every season and emotion: joy, grief, fear, hope, weariness, gratitude, and praise, reminding us that God meets us in each one.

Whether you have time for deep study or only a short moment before the day begins, this study offers rich devotionals, biblical insight, and intentional reflection to help you grow in Scripture and draw near to Jesus.

Sit down with the Savior and discover how Jesus is revealed throughout the Psalms while finding encouragement for busy and spiritually weary seasons. As you spend time in God's Word, you'll learn practical ways to stay rooted in Scripture, grow in confidence in understanding and applying the Bible, and deepen your affection for the God who meets you with grace.

We don't need perfect routines or hours of free time to experience the beauty of God's Word. We simply need a willing heart. So let's open our Bibles, bring our twenty minutes, and encounter Jesus through the songs He knew and loved.

About the Author

Kristin Nave loves helping people understand, love, and apply the Bible to their lives. She's the host of the *Love the Bible* podcast and is the author of Bible studies. Kristin speaks at women's conferences, churches, and her Bible study workshops, equipping others to go deeper in God's Word. She loves sharing Bible insights and tools through social media and everyday life. Kristin holds a M.A. in Biblical studies, and lives in California with her husband and teenage daughter.

From the Publisher

GREAT STUDIES

ARE EVEN BETTER WHEN THEY'RE SHARED!

Help others find this study:

- Post a review at your favorite online bookseller.
- Post a picture on a social media account and share why you enjoyed it.
- Send a note to a friend who would also love it—or, better yet, go through it with them.

Thanks for helping others grow their faith!